A Northern Habitat

Collected Poems
 1960–2010

Robin Fulton Macpherson

A Northern Habitat

Collected Poems
1960–2010

Robin Fulton Macpherson

MARICK PRESS

LIBRARY OF CONGRESS CATALOGUING
IN PUBLICATION DATA
Fulton Macpherson, Robin
Collected Poems. English.
A Northern Habitat/Robin Fulton Macpherson
ISBN: 978-1-934851-47-0

Copyright © 2013 by Robin Fulton Macpherson
Copyright © 2013 Marick Press

Edited by Mariela Griffor, Travis Denton, & the Author

Design and typesetting by HSDesigns
Cover design by HSDesigns
Cover Image: Dorothy Stirling
Printed and bound in the United States.

Marick Press
P.O. Box 36253
Grosse Pointe Farms
Michigan 48236
www.marickpress.com

Distributed by spdbooks.org and Ingram

MARICK PRESS

To LISE

CONTENTS

I

EARLY POEMS (1960-1969)

Clear Morning on a Hill   23
Elements of Christmas   24
Deer   25
An Old Woman at the Window   26
The End of an Age   27
In Memoriam Alberto Giacometti   28
Corruption of Winter   29
In Spite of the Season   30
Gardenwork   31
Close   32
November Clown   33
All at Once   34
Remote   35

From THE SPACES BETWEEN THE STONES (1971)

It Takes a Rare Person   39
Describing a City   40
Forecast for a Quiet Night   41
White   42
Anxieties of an Insider   43
from Variations on a Pine-Tree   44
from The Spaces between the Stones   46
Those who Wait   49
The Music of the Spheres   50

From THE MAN WITH THE SURBAHAR (1971)

Hung Red 55
From Interiors without Walls 64
From The Cold Musician 67
From Songs for a Cool Man 70
From The Voice of the Surbahar 72

From TREE-LINES (1974)

Four Poems from Assynt 79
A Northern Habitat 83
Underwater 86
Rain 88
Passing the Somme 90
In Mariefred 91
From Certain Angles 93
In Memoriam Antonius Block 94

From SELECTED POEMS 1963-1978 (1980)
and FIELDS OF FOCUS (1982)

The Change 107
Passing Events 108
In Touch 109
Outlook 110
Museums and Journeys 111
Visingsö 112
Midsummer Nights 113
Runmarö 114
Revelations 115
A Tree Alone 116
Remembering an Island 117
Night-Music 118
A Fifteenth Century Triptych 119

The Waiting Room 122
Travelling North in Spring 123
Travelling Alone 124
Things that Last 125
Reading Lagerkvist on the Day he Died 126
Waking in the Small Hours 127
Home Thoughts 128
Listening to Rachmaninov in a New House 129
Stopping by Shadows 130
Resolutions 131
After a Journey to a New Found Land 132
Music and Flight 133
Birthdays 134
Coming Back 135
Light from the North 136
Something like a Sky 137
Ancient Timber 138
Safe Mornings 139
Something We Didn't Know Was There 140
In Memoriam. Again 141
Hot Days in Cambridge 142
Night Alone 143
Notes for a Summer 144
Travelling 145
Marazion 146
Elegies 147
Places to Stay In 148
The Manse 150
Turning Forty 151
Keeping Steady 152
What to Do with the Word "Home"? 153
A Night and a Morning 154
Flying over Arran 155
East Coast Revisited 156
From 1939 157
On an Etching of Dedham Vale by Glynn Thomas 158
Undated Photograph 159

11

Following a Mirror   160
Loss of Outlook   161
Edges   162
Hurrying in Spring   163
Passing Verdun   164
Note for a Japanese Poet   165
Listening to a Curlew   166
Finds, circa 1948   168
A Photo, a Clock   169
Revisiting a Clock 170
Reading a Page   171
Remembering Walls   172
Walking in Woods   173

From COMING DOWN TO EARTH AND SPRING IS SOON (1990)

Arriving by Train, December   177
The Swing Bridge   178
Railway Embankments   179
Home Ground   180
Alive Again   181
Almost a Habit   182
On Not Saying Much   183
Shostakovitch Opus 138   184
To an English Composer   185
The Story of Kaspar Hauser   186
Grass   187
Winter Trains   188
Not Lost   189
Just after the Shortest Day   190
Wakeful, Thirty Years Ago   191
A Jewish Cemetery   193
Travelling, to an Old Place   194
Multitudes   195
Infra-Red Photograph   196
Messages in Spring   197

Morning Words   198
Time-Keepers   199
Reaching Lübeck   200
Easter Sunday Windows   201
Lasting   202
Requiem   203
During a Final Illness   204
What the Colours Said   205
Languages   206
Two Pictures on my Wall   207
Visiting Your Death   208
Homage to a Gardener   210
Not Yet   211
Unquiet Highland Landscape   212
Noon Standstill   213
Cloud and Seed   214
Marrel Hill   215
Last Views   216
Wood Fire and Summer Rain   217
In My Dream   218
Mårup Church   219
Can't Stop   220
August 1920   221
Travelling South, Looking North   223
Tide   224
Landscape with Verticals   225
A False Dream   226
The Green Boat, the Night Wind and the Birch   227

UNCOLLECTED 1976-1990

A Word for a Word   231
Things Coming Back   233
Arran Haiku   234
After Ash Wednesday   235
Good Friday in Einbeck   236
The Dead in Dreams   237

He Has Come Back   238
The Three of Us   239

II

POEMS 1988-2010

For Something like a Second   243
Childhood   244
Garden   245
Helmsdale   246
Family   247
One of Our Present Tenses   248
The Bell   249
Icon   250
The Watermark   251
I Take my Way Back   252
Perfectionists   253
Looking West from Hå   254
My Rivers   255
Autumn Storm   257
Those Who'll Stay   258
Shostakovitch Opus 122   259
Shostakovitch Opus 144   260
Britten's *Lachrymae*   261
One-Part Invention   262
Two-Part Invention   263
Three-Part Invention   264
The Inheritance   265
Relearning Russian   266
Highland Pebble   267
Windows   268
Heights   269
Vaughan Williams - One of his Tunes   270
Strath   271

The Village   272
Native Land   273
Verdun   274
Home Thoughts   275
Equinox   276
From a History of Music   277
Thurso, July 1947   278
Small World   279
Five-Finger Nocturne   280
Inside History   281
Setting Out   282
On the Other Side of Language   283
Inside the Spacious Tomb   284
Good Friday in the Fields of Denmark   285
Early May   286
Summer in the Mountains   287
Between Hanseatic Facades   288
Old Edinburgh Facades   289
Living-Space   290
Travelling on All Saints' Day   291
Welcoming Swifts   292
A Clear Start to the Day   293
Crossing into November   294
Praise   295
The History of a Morning   296
A Symphony Begins   297
Closing Scene   298
Crossing April on Foot   299
Torches   300
Looking at Midsummer   301
Flensburg Spire   302
In Picardy   303
New House Made Old   304
Birches   305
Facing Night   306
Find   307
Notes on the Laws of Nature   308

Our Alphabet 309
Genealogy 310
Daylight 311
Night Vision 312
Their Houses 313
At the Mercy of Secret Machines 314
Flight Levels 315
Sunlight 316
Going Away and Coming Back 317
On TV 318
The Saw-Player 319
I Give Back Some Brightness 320
From a Summer Journey 321
Large Questions 322
A Version of Me 323
Listening In 324
Dusk 325
Tree in Spring 326
The Sea's Openness 327
Proving 328
Nocturnal 329
A Simile for William Crozier 330
Thatched Roofs at Night 331
By the Ely Road 332
Elm Tree in February 333
From a High Window 334
Local History 335
Memorial 337
Ancient Stones Visit Us 338
In My Own Company 339
Something Stubborn 340
The Names 341
Nightfall in St Mary's Lane 342
A Balloon Perhaps 343
Civilisation 344
Visit 345
Looking at Earth 346

News Reaches a Translator   347
Waiting to Cross a Fjord   348
Forty-Two Years   349
Passing the Borders   350
Having Crossed the Skagerrak   351
Entering a Forest   353
On the Death of Werner Aspenström   354
A Dream, a White Wall   355
After Six Decades   356
On a Birthday   357
Small World   358
Cathedral   359
Breath   360
Inspection   361
Shadow   362
Sightings   363
Buying a Map   365
Rhododendron Opening   366
On a Summer's Day   367
This Time   368
About to Leave an Island   369
Navigation   370
Birch in July   371
Paint   372
Walking into a Cold Wind   373
Stopping for the Night   374
Acorn   375
Rock   376
Consolation   377
In Adam House   378
Gale   379
Watercolour   380
Forest Mirror   381
Fathoms   382
Ocean Dream   383
Two Trees   384
November Report   385

We'll Listen   386
Sparrow   387
Blue Trees   388
Glass   389
Still Life   390
Geography Lessons   391
The Weight of Light   392
Willow-Herb   393
Fugue   394
A Bookcase, Emptied   395
Emigrant Ships   396
After a Phone Call   397
Undoing a Picture   398
Looking at Paint   399
In Schleswig   400
At the Photo-Copier   401
From a Landscape in April   402
Log Entry   403
Music from 1724   404
Minster   405
Winter Mornings   406
Light Years   407
The Words for Trees   408
Black Harris Tweed   409
Of Night   410
The Road   411
On Deck at Night   412
A Photo of Life and Art   413
August the Fourth Begins   414
September Levels   415
Gathering Apples   416
New Lives   417
Postcard   418
On a Late Sonata   419
Evolution   420
Sycamore and Broom   421
The River   422

A Picture   423
Flemsøya   424
August Evening on Deck   425
Beneath a Boat-Shaped Moon   426
Rust   427
Homing I-X   428
Mist   434
Weather Cock   435
Field in Spring   436
In York Minster   437
Distances   438
Spring Gale   439
Reaching Helmsdale   440
Sycamores   442
A Kind of Clearance   443
Dutch, 17th Century   444
In Fairfax Street   445
On an Old Pavement   446
Back Door   447
October Dusk   448
Octet   449
Cathedrals Afloat   450
The Knowledge   451
Hurricane   452
Interior   453
A Change Coming   454
Above Dover Beach   455
Grass   456
Late   457
Apart from Anything Else   458
Low Watt Would Do   459
Spring Morning   460
As In   461
Shared Cloud   462
Names I've Lost   463
The Colours of Night   464
Looking Up   465

Rain   466
Border-Crossing   467
Dipper   468
Gladiolus   469
Loss   470
Words like Trout   471
Whitsun   472
The Grassmarket, Overcrowded   473
Things on their Way   474
Passer Domesticus   475
Actress in a Bad Garden   476
Wood Anemone   477
A Late Quartet   478
The Prow   479
1943   480
1948   481
1953   482
First Light   483
Leaving   484
A Homecoming   485
Hawthorn   486
Such Blue and Yellow   487
Centenary   488
The Bell   489
Living Where   490
Cloudless   491
At Last   492
Hearing the Sea   493
A Day Impaired   494
Standstill   495
January Freeze   496
Window   497
Aldeburgh Perhaps   498

Notes   499

EARLY POEMS
(1960-1969)

I

CLEAR MORNING ON A HILL

Shape comes with light. The hill
with clear edges becomes high:
moss, with is own edges and tiny
shadows, becomes what moss is.

A man, himself clear in the light,
imagines hill upon hill upon hill,
builds them from, sinks them to
the one hill under his feet.

The light adds nothing but itself
yet will make the hill simple
and heavy, the moss intricate,
long after the man has carried
his unsteady hills away.

ELEMENTS OF CHRISTMAS

The elements are always there: water and straw,
beasts with warm noses and ignorant eyes,
shepherds satisfied that they have found
another myth, wise men who trace
to its source whatever bright notion falls
from their Babylonian sky; at the centre rests
the everlasting family set-piece
and in the distance Herod dreams of his enemies' ghosts.

Here, outside this local
window, little sticks
(like gravestones) mark where under snow
tulip-bulbs save up and nourish
blood-red secrets which at Easter will overflow.

DEER

If God had stood there, high-antlered,
eyes jewelled for a second, fearful of
my car's predatory noise yet giving
cold appraisal from the edge of the flowing road -

(there were white lines to follow, nothing clear
except my own lights exploding forward,
all meaning narrowed between verges) -
if God, would the beast in Him have fled?

AN OLD WOMAN AT THE WINDOW

The thunder has lost its memory
but it goes on mumbling,

fish in their element
leap, an alien light.

Heavy raindrops echo
in a deep well.

Cover the mirror and sit back
and watch.

THE END OF AN AGE

The chestnut they said had stood for seventy years.
Its whiteness in May, redness in September,
thin scrolls of long fingery twigs,
were things expected of it.
The tree was an obvious landmark, like a hill.

The little people hurrying about the place,
their heads packed with intricacies,
their feet not in the habit of standing still,
slightly envied the tree
for adding such tiny cubits to itself.

At last, for safety's sake it had to come
and, falling, for the first time became heavy.
A man with an axe sorting it all out
but making slow work
said "A tree's complicated when it's down."

IN MEMORIAM ALBERTO GIACOMETTI

"The more you pare the fatter it becomes" -
by which you meant, I suppose, that leanness
occupies its space exactly.
You pressed matter to vanishing point.
Your fingers restlessly expunged
the most tenuous superfluity.

There is a limit, though, which now you've passed:
not to be at all is an extreme.

For us your existences are large,
massive between slender definitions.

CORRUPTION OF WINTER
(after Innokentii Annenskii)

Spring's dull chilly eye
is on the land, sombrely
new mourners leave the new grave
dusting snow like breadcrumbs from their coats.

Winter is corruption now,
poured through channels, down
drains, softened and spread into acres of filth
and rottenness of last year's unburied growth.

Ditches are brimmed with the stuff.
It even finds a way beneath
shuttered windows till you'd hardly think
the green stubble of life could prick through.

The road to heaven, they say, is mud.
What kind of children can come
from the marriage of a dead man, a dead season?
Fledglings in the elm jerk and complain.

IN SPITE OF THE SEASON
(after a story by Yurii Kazakov)

Things have been going too well.
Must hold steady. Don't
stare at the river-boat.
Arrival's a precarious thing.

She comes. The river at home
is now a black crack in the ice,
the sea is weighed down with floes.
In summer there we speared bass.

When I left she said "Why?
Going south is going forever."
Now her White Sea voice
is rough and intimate again.

All night through at the fire.
All morning asleep. Then:
snow - winter has caught up,
the woods of oak and larch are bare.

At my window she waits
while I take the water-can.
White earth, blue air.
Bubbles scamper in the creaking ice.

How bright for a dead season!
Things have been going too well.
Up the soft path I strain
to hold the live and kicking water still.

GARDENWORK
(after S I Kirsanov)

Speech is a winterhardy class. I've
taken to heart my hybridology:
you will always find me hunched up
eyes narrowed over wordstalks.

For some it's generous September,
free mushrooms in the autumn woods.
For me it's a linguistic herbarium,
a forestful of singular voices.

Stiff frost silvers a twig hard,
clinging slush softly chokes it -
my graft takes on and here's a new strain,
unique berry, personal-appletree.

Across ten thousand acres my crop
of words is dense. After the first year
already there are giant melonouns
and the lucky branches are heavy with
                plumbrageous verbs.

CLOSE

A God-fearing rule-
of-thumb existence,
two generations back.

My ways were exotic.
We had to talk simply
not about what "mattered."

Weather mostly. He was
a drystone dyke
whose rough parts fit
delicately and not even
the wind can prise them open.

NOVEMBER CLOWN

Treading lightly on the trodden path,
poppies in his hair and shining
phosphorescent bones and tattered skin -
"gold pennies for your eyes,
little silences on the battlefield..."

He seems childish but his touch burns
and playfully he has touched all of us.

ALL AT ONCE

Suddenly
running through a large house
with all the windows and doors open -
the landscape has disappeared!

There is no-one to wave to.
No air to carry your words.
All at once
the freedom you spent a lifetime for!

You would willingly spend another
to put a branch back on a tree,
to close a door,
to stumble on a difficult word.

REMOTE

Though far it's not difficult to reach,
twenty miles from a remote village
then a three-mile trudge on the moor
(it feels like climbing a steep hill that's on the level).

There are rancid pools and green soft-spots
and small sticky plants that eat flies.
On the slopes deer pause, cautiously
aware of the wooden creature crawling on the loch.

It's not difficult to stay, passive
to the heathery wind and summer rain, curious
about the age of wiry bits of trees
preserved in peat-banks the water is hollowing out.

Leaving such a place behind you
is another matter. Into the northern dusk
you hump your stiff trout and stiff bones
and what you half believe is a wiser sense of time.

You have also found a new prison for the mind.
It is always open.
You have bad dreams about the frantic rower
cruelly enclosed by the vast space he's in.

from
THE SPACES BETWEEN THE STONES
(1973)

IT TAKES A RARE PERSON
(like Iain Crichton Smith)

Soft clouds
and the green spaces are soft and green.
The local gods have stone hearts,
there is green mould on the rocks.

Black fruit:
laws of an ancient desert people,
of grandfathers still gazing
smudged and brown from the mantelpiece
sharing the honours with the youngster smudged at Loos.

A stony grip
on heaven, a stony eye on those
who mix pleasure with pure spirit,
the new generation and the old
clichés and the turning of backs.

It takes
a rare person to look through stones
to the other side, to see blood in them,
to see gods with glassy minds shining
in a hard light that knows how to touch gently.

DESCRIBING A CITY
(Sheffield, mid 1960s)

    1

I shall not name your parts for your parts and their names are
   changing.

    2

I could describe: the language of signs I used so that I didn't get lost
but the signs changed and I had to learn daily improvisation
and I did get lost both entering and leaving and living in the forest
of doubtful images, of worn paths that led to broken squares.

I could describe: my daily work, a glossary at hand, a view
of collegiate trees, but the words I learned have had to be changed
and my notes are now cumbersome.

    3

       I shall describe: a broken square
of uneven foundations, crushed bricks, dandelions,
with a neat but old road round it and thin veteran streetlamps
that faithfully each night illumine odd patches of nothing,
and half along one side a pub with jagged edges is left
whose customers still hobble faithfully over the broken bricks.
I shall describe: another square waiting its chance, a house not
habitable but inhabited by a bed-ridden face that stared
daily at me as I walked by, at me trying not to think
of furry bits of history with teeth and eyes and smooth tails
and enough cunning to follow me and keep me in sight from a safe
   distance.

FORECAST FOR A QUIET NIGHT

A secret cone will drop in Rothiemurcus.
A quiet wind will stroke Loch Araichlin.

By dawn imperceptible frosty wrinkles
will have puckered the edges of countless backwaters.

By dawn too a generation of mice
will have been snipped by a night-shift of owls
working separately and almost in silence.

And the mild local disturbance behind the eyes
of the invalid
will have been noted only by the next of kin.

WHITE

A memory:
a white stone in six inches of water.
Because it burns a white hole in your mind,
because it's so near the surface it offends you,
you reach for it to throw it into the depths.

You reach through and through and through.
For the rest of your life will you be obsessed by six fathomless inches?

ANXIETIES OF AN INSIDER

My ceiling is blue as the sky is supposed to be.
The walls are yellow (that's the golden earth).
The pictures show allegorical trees
where the happy ones contemplate in rows
and not a single leaf is frayed.
The windows are painted to match the colours
                                      of my eyes.

Why do you come here with grey thoughts?
Let them settle and reflect my blue ceiling.
Why do you bring a stony silence with you?
Let it melt in the yellow shade of my walls.
Why do you stand pointing like that?
Let my eyes be the window on your world.

You finger my brittle preserved flowers.
You remark on the hairfine cracks in the paint,
on the spiders waiting on assymetrical webs
(they're schizophrenic, you say, let them be).
I am waiting for you to go away. Why
do you stare at me through a white bandage
                                        of light?

from VARIATIONS ON A PINE-TREE

2

The tree knows its position and clings to it:
I am a crowd stumbling, stooping, squinting.
There is no position the tree can call its own:
my endless variations on its theme
cluster round a theme that isn't there.

3

I walk round the tree slowly:
three hundred and sixty appearances
all two-dimensional still-lives.
I hold them sideways, the tree disappears.
I flick through them, the tree waves its arms.
I have mastered the tree's appearances.

4

A squirrel sprints up and down:
it too robs the tree
of one dimension, it runs along
ground and bole and ground
in an athletic straight line.

5

The tree acts,
knows to perfection his one role.
I act un-
certainly this role and that
perpetually on the point of falling.

6

It is a muscular stance.
Here and now I too can stiffly pose
but only by imitating the wooden master.

7

The tree leans, he
is about to move, he
has achieved a rigid balance between
moving and not moving, earth and air.

11

Does the tree ever dream?
Does it wish the poised deer
were wooden, to poise forever?

12

Does the tree sometimes dream he is God
commanding attention by standing still,
creaking now and again and sighing
and giving the interpreters much worry?

13

What resinous ghost inhabits
this bony wooden machine?
Rap the wood and the wood raps.

14

To be dismembered in straight cuts:
a sweet haze, the ghost escapes.

from THE SPACES BETWEEN THE STONES

1

We clear spaces between the stones.
The stones resist.
What will we plant between the stones?
The roots resist.
The flowers are stone-hard between the stones.

2

The stones hold spaces open for us.
Here is an arrow-slit for pinning down
crawling enemies on the plain below,
now a narrow picture-postcard of farms
and an edge of cold on the leaning face.

4

The grey stones of the kirk walls
clutch each other with a dying grasp.
They hunch their backs to the east wind.
Out of the wind
the congregation listens
to the slow drop of pebbles one
by one slipped from the everlasting hands.

5

Men in yellow helmets
are picking the stones apart.
We can look through the walls
at the hearth in mid-air.
The stones are being forced:
their secrets are carried away in jagged lumps.
There is nothing left in the spaces between the stones.

6

We clear spaces between the stones.
The stones grow and fill the spaces.

9

The stones crush the feet that walk on them.
The generations are crossing the stones for ever.
The green fields on the far side of the desert
are not there.
Here where the generations have been crushed
it is green for a time.
The spaces between the stones are for sap to gather.

10

The spaces between the stones are crushed.
The stones resist.
The stones are crushed.
Slowly a ribbon of new road is laid.

11

Stones with straight edges fit together.
Man-made stones have straight edges.

If only men had straight edges, they'd fit.
We've seen the politics of straight edges.

The spaces between the stones are patrolled and wired.
Between the stones words have no shadows.

12

The new spaces are not between the stones.
The new spaces are inside the stones.

Columbus sails on nothing, a multi-million-
to-one chance of striking a particle.

The edge of the world is now wherever we choose
to fall off, the edge is everywhere.

Here is a space the stones can never close.
We have now entered the stones.
They're empty.
Tiny sparks make a universe of their own.

    13

Here is a man
who can disintegrate the rim of the world
by picking the lock at the small still centre.

Here is a man
a weightless man clutching his weightless faith
in the love that moves the sun and the other stars.

Here is a man
who is learning the rules of weightlessness
who is seeing the green valleys for the first time.

Here is a man
who is learning a new way between the stones.
The spaces between the stones are full of light.

THOSE WHO WAIT

You've seen Dürer's "Melancholia:"
the sphere and the dodecahedron wait,
in the limp hand the compasses describe nothing.
When melancholy wakes an army moves
with a million tools in good order.
We watch the huge skies inside an atom.
The hungry people have spikes of glass in their eyes.

The steel falcons wait outside.
The radar turns his eye turns his eye.
At her finger enough fire-power
to skin a continent alive.
She waits.
She knows the answer. She's not afraid.
She can't lift her finger in the heavy air.

Her minions are restless.
Our printed circuits, instantaneous news,
the world is a green marble in the palm of her hand.
The broken people wait to be made whole.
The whole people know they will soon be broken.
Why does she wait? She is bored
by the clouds that dull her silver landscape.

THE MUSIC OF THE SPHERES

1

"Music please!" And the man at the telescope
looks and listens, looks and listens and waits.
This vulgar Beethoven is thrust
like a crude vase on the mind's mantelpiece
to interrupt the monotony of space:
pastoral valleys in a calculating brain,
green waters to catch a falling star.

What the old German scratched on paper
was, though, true
of the giant nebulae that rolled away
past him into his green and silent night.

2

It's only at the last centimetre
where music is made.

Ptolemy's little golden wheels
will shine for ever, they are laid
and numbered in silk-lined boxes.
In their time
they were the movement of God's brain
smoothly timeless in their jewelled bearings.

The spheres are broken and their music
is war.
They do not keep time with each other
for time bends.

It is vain to cloud the sky over
with coarse noise to cheat the silence
for the silence slips through,

a ghost of dust.
It's only at the last centimetre
where there's space enough for music
and for me to walk about in it listening.

    3

If they do
catch creation in the act,
if they do
reach an edge that is really an edge
and not just the edge of their minds,
if they do
trace time and space into
a new multifoliate rose,

I'd like to stand at the last centimetre
where the long ellipses touch down
and listen
to the old music taking the strain of the new
and putting out notes like snowdrops
as if
there had been no crushing weight of winter.

from THE MAN WITH THE SURBAHAR
   (1971)

HUNG RED

    1

A political act? Art?
A communal distraction?
We come in out of the dark
and in the blinding white room
our grey faces and black
coats look apologetic.

The bright red actors
possibly he and she
with no eyes or mouths
circle and struggle and claw
within the cramped limits
of an imaginary prison.

They keep to the centre of the room.
There's a safe distance between
that threatens to be suddenly fatal:
an imaginary prison
can expand at will and they
would invite us in.

We hold our breath,
wish we weren't here.
We press back to the wall,
wish we were white paper
that would cling to the wall and become
for the duration invisible.

    2

Our world stops at the window. We hear an owl:
he has his own ways of seeing in the dark,
he himself is opaque, his screams fall like stones.

The blue light of the TV stares through us.
We have learned to unread what the voices say.
The images are true, the justifications false.

The signal is weak. Snow falls on the burning huts.
Children at bayonet practice, pilots dazed by sun,
the faces turn white with black edges.

The images are true because the actors are bad.
The president can raise an eyebrow and smile
but his victim burns clumsily, unconvincingly.

People running on the TV screen are opaque.
The blue eye is staring through us, its world
has no windows, we are all looking out and in.

Switch the eye off, the images are still true.
We walk about the room, transparent bodies,
our heads fine networks of ice-clear blood.

Our eyes are blue, we stare through each other.
Our world stops at the window, at our reflections.
Dark specks are falling through us, black snow.

    3

"Hold a glass of pure water to the eye of the sun."
The sun will scorch your retina, a merciless razor.
Hold up a glass of the Mekong or the Jordan.
The eye of the sun will be safe now, only a glimmer
in the cloudy element, our substitute for daylight.
The cloud preys on itself yet the cloud survives
always at the cost of those who do not survive.
The water of the Ganges is also cloudy. What kind
of cleanliness justifies the wet pilgrims?
There's scum on the naked eye. Don't trust the eye.

4

Like a leaf
held to the eye of the sun, miraculous veins.
On the white wall the shadow is opaque and black.

Like us
transparent in all weathers to the naked eye,
infinite ramifications, maximum exposure.

Like our
shadows, tight-lipped, enigmatic, negotiating
for us with the shadows of presidents.

Unlike us
these are indifferent, would still be opaque
if they failed and we hung on, paper skeletons.

5

You pull back the red curtains of your mind.
Your face is like the moon
whose burning deserts look cold in the night.

Your eyes have the blue flicker of a TV screen
whose images slip and hold:
you see through the dark mercilessly.

I am a brief shadow, a disturbance
between two words,
I fall from the sky, am shot, explain myself.

Your eyes are indifferent. The president is speaking
but fear not, the flames
between his words are distant, silvery, cool.

While I, in the darkness which hides nothing,
flare out like a match
struck but invisible in the sun.

      6

A ghost of Europe, a Gutenberg zombie with four
of his senses gone and a mist of print on his eyes.
When all he can do is see, what is there left to see?
The words teem like the microscopic life in water
simultaneously coupling murdering multiplying
or like the TV images of his flat universe
where the president's words are invisible and silent
and the peasant is burned alive and painlessly.

The skin on his eyes thickens. He forgets the sun
and fumbles his way around the new world
like someone struggling with braille but finding it beyond him.

      7

Your mind is a small square white room
so bright that the naked eye weeps.
Scarlet curtains hang where windows should be.
The table has nothing on it, the chair is empty.

You approach with your written request,
knock and wait,
knowing that an answer would be blinding
and must in due process come.

      8

The eye of the distant loch
never closes,
it reflects and suffers all
but sees nothing,

it gives you an eye for an eye
and you see only yourself.

Hell is an open mind
that never closes
but reflects and suffers all
and sees nothing.
The soft nerves are torn
and always heal.

Hell is an open mind
that prays for:
ice on the camera lens,
scum on the eye,
snow on the TV screen
and an end to eternity.

    9

Why do they blindfold people about to be shot?
To shield their eyes from the impact of eternity?
(As safe as bits of coloured glass to look through
at the next nuclear bomb.) No, it's to shield the eyes
of those who are taking aim at a blindfolded object.

To look at the eyes of a man you're about to shoot
would be like staring at the sun with a glass
of water (pure water) acting as a magnifier
and long before he was dead he would be scorched
to an ashy silhouette on the grey wall at the back of your head.

    10

The presidents all shake hands.
Their hands have the same temperature.
The diplomats raise glasses.
Their eyes twinkle in the pure water.

The ministers divide an ocean,
say, "Who'll drown in a saucer?
Look, the willow-pattern shows
through, the world wobbles in our fingers!"

There is much talk of pure blood.
Hold a glass to the eye of the sun:
what's going on in there
is a clip from a horror film.

"The containment and spilling of blood
is the concern of the chosen few
who stand like cut-outs and worry -
Could the domino theory be true?"

Keep the trade figures burning
from ticker tape to geography text:
Denmark is noted for bacon, first
catch your pig and cure it.

The ghost of Prince Hamlet spits
in the wishing well.
With a smile he removes his right eye
and offers it in a nutshell.

11

The TV screen is always accommodating.
Even when switched off it is never blank, as now
you waddle and bulge like an orange clown
in a square room that strains to be circular.

With a clear view of appearances you look out:
people are walking like ghosts in a comic
tugging at the awkward white sheets
draped clumsily from identical domed heads.

Hard to imagine how they see where they're going
or how the appearance of a clear morning
can be maintained. Can no-one see a soft black
snow distilled from the blue air

charred flakes that look too heavy to float
drifting and hesitating like thin doubtful leaves?
Their touch is soft and the white hurrying people,
who don't see them, carry spreading grey stains.

You never thought that walls could be insubstantial
as they are now, or that you'd curse your clear
view of appearances when you observe the stains
seeping into your newly transparent body
not grey but poisonous with a rainbow of colours.

   12

There is still a red eye watching us
through the clouds.
The rain will never wash its reflection away
even from the dark streets.

If the eye were rock like the faces of Liathach
we could understand
its hardness and age, but the eye that never shuts
we can never understand.

In the small white rooms of our mind the red
light is suffused
evenly illuminating nothing but itself.
The mind's eye is inflamed.

Hell is an open mind that never closes
even in the dark,
is also a closed mind that never opens.
A fine acid drizzle falls on them both.

13

Before they grow dull and look back like strangers,
before they look past me to the white horizon,
before I turn away when the light hurts -

against that tenderness I could break
these clenched words like crumbling rock.

14

In a white light in a white room
on a white scaffold hung - red

red what?

Longer and thinner than people (a skinned
person still resembles a person);
only an ideal could be hung
so glaringly.

An ideal Europe. The sad
particulars have been taken down
from lamp-posts and barbed wire
and other positions of authority.

The ideal is always bright.
Europe was a series of grey corners
and most of the millions who bled in them
did so in shadows.

You are free to walk out of the room.
You are free (at the moment) to step
through the white walls of Europe
but not through the white walls of your mind.

Beautiful abstract shadows wait

behind each nervous particular:
become a white silhouette
on a white wall, or be hung - red.

from INTERIORS WITHOUT WALLS

    1

The leaves have fallen and the woods are empty,
our white walls are open to the new snow
and we are at the mercy of clouds hurrying past.
What do they hide? What will fall from them?

We know too much, have learned how ghosts walk
without obstacles, through the red wall
of our empire, the black wall of our heart,
the shimmering blue curtains of our innocence.

Our thoughts taste of hard November mornings.
How cool. We shiver with anticipation
after the brown mess of the seasons. No,
we're too young to have minds with an edge of ice.

If our minds were all ice there would be no end
to our mastery, no fear of clouds,
no anger at the red wall, no pity
for the black, no sorrow for the torn curtain

and at last with our glazed eyes wide open
and seeing everything we would lie down
totally exposed, totally locked away
between the thick layers of two geological eras.

    2

There is always a cold wind from frozen edges,
always rumours of icemen in the mountains
and of border tribes who have taught themselves
never to close their eyes.

All that is somewhere in our history books

whose thin pages are pecked by articulate crows
who mistake pure thoughts for bloodstains
and bore us with "We told you so, we told you so!"

Truth is easy on a cold morning. Water
hangs in spikes, shadows have white edges.
Feelings people had yesterday are rigid
like a family staring at an early camera.

Newly discovered edges are creeping inwards
and the notices put up get nearer and nearer:
"Keep off the poisoned grass!
The frozen edge of the mind is slippery!"

Exposure beyond window-frames and doorways:
eyes narrow at what is happening in the distance,
eyes widen at what is whispered in ears
and echoes as far as the mountains.

6

They dance to a song about a gently weeping guitar.

They gather cold green apples at the end of autumn
(perhaps winter and spring will have a bitter taste)
they keep warm stooping among the bare trees.

They look past each other at the white shadows
(perhaps winter will hem them in with black edges)
they breathe warmly on the first soft flakes that fall.

They hear the wind rising between their sentences
(perhaps winter will leave nothing to say in spring)
when the song ends they carry on dancing gently.

I eavesdrop among their words and imaginings.
I hear the welling

of an almost silent breaker shouldering
between the stanchions of a pier at night.

    7

In the distance between two standing close
something remote happens.

They lose each other in brown desolation
streaked by the first white
scars of winter howling in from the edges.
They stumble away from each other
with no sense of direction conscious only
of total exposure between
sky and earth, and the minimal life at their feet
shudders in scratchy lumps
beneath wind battering for wider lebensraum.

What can they do, ambushed from within?
Their voices are frayed to nothing.
The very idea of a word trying to speak out there,
of a soft word surviving,
is like waking in the wrong geological age.
Their clothes are too thin,
their bones encumbered with skin and nerves
which will soon be frayed also.
They lose their last breath shouting inaudibly.

Everyone else in the room is tipsy and laughing.
It sounds like the rusty cawing
of a high convoy of geese on its trek south.

from THE COLD MUSICIAN

1

An epitaph for the cold musician:
"a few grey stones and many dreams."

His hands are always cold, his world white
with thin black borders to everything
and veils of irridescent harmonics.

The good dreams and the bad are the same:
he's an old tree that has opened a million leaves
in the wrong season. He's a crystal freak.

When he's old perhaps he'll dream of stones
and waking grope for daylight with hands
moist and helpless as leaves in their proper season.

When he's old perhaps his dreams will sound
like the Leonora trumpet. Heaven is always
off-stage, echoing with the voices of the damned
who shout at tall cliffs and hear their own names answer.

2

December dawn, moon and morning star are alone.
Shadows of bare twigs on white walls hardy move.

Luonnotar - this music is aeons colder
than surburban frost that makes children hurry.
How cold was creation? Only the cold survive
and she survived, waiting for motherhood.
Her desire must have been harder than ice.

A postcard from Uppsala: trees rigid crystal
and cathedral spire unwavering in its aim.

Heaven is blue for a few hours and always cold.
The will to keep pointing like that must be harder than stone.

    3

"Your feelings are black and white, your music cold.
Your photo on the piano has been staring at you
from its white border and black frame
with the same rigid smile year after year.
 "La fille aux cheveux de lin" in a northern waste
where the few scrub trees grow hunched
and the night air is sour with frost and salt:
she would have died young and unnoticed."

"I play well when my hands are cold. I bask
in the soft irridescences of hard ice."

    7

To admit to nervous fictions:

"My arpeggios trip
on an untuned string
with a cloudy twang.
My freakish geranium
has stretched too tall
and is now ready to topple.
The photo of my dead friend
has scowled more and more
since the day he smiled and died.
There is no pity.
My magical invisible tower
of spinning plates and hoops
is a dead weight.
How long can I
with a slim flourish deceive
my blind and deaf admirers?

They would never forgive
a twang, a topple, a scowl."

"The musician is cold
yet his music warms us all."

If the fiction breaks will the truth
be any less nervous?

from SONGS FOR A COOL MAN

1

I can't take it cool any more, the icicles burn,
                the snow on my hand hurts.
I've lived in a foursquare house in a foursquare
                garden carved with frost.
I've heard the steps behind walls, I promise I
                haven't listened at locked doors.
I've read what was written, I've turned a blind eye
                to what was between the lines.
I've been a glass man with a glass god shining in
                my trembling eye.
I've measured my walls my words my music to see
                that they fit without spilling over.
I've measured what I can of the news outside
                to see that it won't trickle in.
The silence is golden, edged by golden sounds,
                desire by ideas of desire.

The icicles tinkle. I open the window. The soft rain
                burns holes in my skin.

5

Let them in first, the cold man with resinous
                thoughts, the cold woman
who dreams all night of warning lights rising and
                falling at the edge of the sea,
the cold man who weeps if he sees a flower and
                scowls if someone offers it to him,
the cold woman who takes what she's given and
                locks it away for ever and ever,
the cold man who hides behind warm words and
                looks desperately out
at the cold woman whose warm words say I'm
                cold enough already stay away.

The long queues of cold people huddled under
                the posters that instruct
how to spend money they haven't got keeping
                the warmth they've never had.

The cold kingdom to come, the cold will that always
                gets its way on earth.

Let them in first, wait, make sure there are no
                voices left in the cities, then follow.

    7

Keep a watch on the windows, look at the world
               through sliding raindrops.
Count your words, use small numbers for
                measuring the immeasurable.
Breathe slowly in the poisoned garden, repeat to
            yourself that stones are stones are stones.
Stand on your own roots if you can, if you can't,
                grope for someone else's.
Take your turn in the cold queue and remind
                yourself your turn will never come.
Beware of overspending yourself when there's
            nothing that love or money can buy.
Don't admit if you can't take it cool any more, if
                they burn you don't cry out.

If you must.

But make sure your silences are loud enough to
           echo and tell us what you're silent about.

from THE VOICE OF THE SURBAHAR

1

It seems a frail mathematics, and ancient,
with an outmoded trust in the beauty of spheres.
But it's not beauty he seeks to make of it
and despite his lonely habits he is no prophet.
His lute is imperfect. If he touches a stone
it is content not to become a fish or a flower
and if trees ever talked to him they've forgotten how.

He imagines: wind meets rockface with a brutish
one plus one equals nothing,
we are at the mercy of complex monsters
training their single red eyes on us.

He imagines the most tender of roots,
the narrowest crack, the most improbable bloom.
The answer is not magic: the right notes
are light and easy, fingers ache on the string.
It's the toughness of a living fibre a child can tear.

At times, in a soft cloud of possibilities
he imagines
the first tentative swing over the edge
of the solar system; they'll stop, listen to the long
extinct bird who is still singing endless ragas.

The musician is dumb and has nervous fingers.
At last after much questioning he writes:
"I try not to look back at her. I try
not to look round at the sun behind me.
Everywhere else I see monuments of salt."

4

You can watch history in the hurrying clouds while
at the back of your mind something keeps knocking
like the wind in a loose window-frame.

Listening to Imrat Khan's Raga Marva,
however often, is not a habit like watching clouds,
more like perpetually and gently waking up
without having first to sleep.

Something at the back of your mind is withered
like the shreds of the pot plant at the window
yet one obsolete bloom suddenly catches the light
and turns transparent for a second or two.

As if a law had come into effect against
hurrying, knocking, withering. There's still doubt
for the raga is described both as "contemplative"
and as "evoking anxiety and restlessness."

The greatest anxiety is in the third section ("jhala")
where you wish the wind would knock louder on the window
to convince you that something at the back of
your mind is still alive but the wish passes indifferent as a cloud

for you know that what's still alive at the back of your mind
is doubt, like an unnecessary flower that never
tires of explaining its necessity, that never
closes its red eye in the dark.

The voice of the surbahar is rich with its own doubt:
a voice that can hesitate without being driven even
by its own rhythm (as clouds are, at the mercy of the wind)
but can, say, in the "alap," pause

to unfold a sentence that hangs in the air like a flower
obeying and at the same time defying
the complex rules of gravity and decay.

    6

I think of Plato
in his everyday form of gardener,
feet scratching on concrete as he lops off
loose ends of summer and his coat-tails
brush drops off nasturtium leaves.
"Thin as water, thick as mercury, they die."
He looks suspiciously at forms that survive.

Raga Sindhu Bhairavi is for mornings
so I walk past the gardener with an easy step.
The loose ends of the music grow in my head
all day but never lose each other
and are never still enough for pure thoughts
to gather and lie in folds like beautiful ice.

    10

At the back of each mind there's a red eye
that never closes and sees through everything.
Its light is inescapable and cruel
unless deflected and divided as the white light
of the sun is divided by a prism

or as the notes of a "rag" are elaborated.
Raga Shree for instance is "very serious"
but when it unfolds like a tree in autumn
there is space and time beneath it
for us to walk about at ease and to see clearly
in its gentle light of many colours.

12

I listen to Raga Marva again. It is said
to be "best suited to performance at sunset"
but here it is in the morning. The northern sun
sends pale level rays. I wear
dark glasses but the world is still bright.

The clear line of the hills is impeccable
with everlasting curves that weary the eye.
The bare branches and innumerable twigs
move only slightly, lightly
unencumbered by the green weight of summer.

I stare at winter. Frost-ferns on windows
melt by noon into smudged rainbows.
The voice of the surbahar, the mind in autumn,
blends and withdraws more deviously,
an improvisation that takes a lifetime to learn.

On the mantelpiece there's an earthenware owl
with two black empty holes for eyes.
He's been staring through me now for years.
No matter who stares back, he never blinks.
Through music he can't hear, he lasts.

from TREE-LINES
(1974)

FOUR POEMS FROM ASSYNT

BY LOCH FEWIN

Nothing to be heard. It's like listening for a note
too low or too high for the human ear
but knowing it's there and the water is so
still it looks solid and transparent.

Nothing to be seen moving but for a cloud-
shadow crossing the rock face of Suilven:
it moves like pure spirit made visible and vanishes
and once more the water is opaque and in motion.

COMING SOUTH FROM LOCH LURGAIN

Morning. Stac Polly is a total wreck, more
total than the puny wreck of a metropolis.
Near the rock a human voice breaks open
like toy thunder, the silence snaps shut on it.

Evening. From the right distance I can see
The Summer Isles levitate above the water
and Cul Beag bright and transparent as a lace
curtain. If I were closer it would ripple in my breath.

THE RED POOL, RIVER KIRKCAIG

Nothing could be less red than this clear water.
I stare through it, my mind clouded with images
of clear water. Boyhood is only six inches
under. I can't reach it, can't see through it.

On the way home I look south to Ben Coigach
whose top is clear for once. The other side of it
drops right down to a fifty fathom hole
off Geodha Mor, scarcely a mile from the shore.

THE NAMES

The hills wear their Gaelic names like old-fashioned hats. Is Meall Dubh no more than a Black Lump? What will happen to a language when it survives only in the names of hills, like the ancient pines in ones and twos, the remains of enveloping forests?

A white boat slides between Isle Martin and Aird Point: the casual English voices echo across the water almost as loud as the calling of migrating geese. By the roadside a telephone-pole whitened by many winters has been singing all day.

In an inlet on the north shore of Loch Assynt I saw a half-sunk rowing boat. Its lines were still visible and it looked as if it might be good enough to retrieve, though perhaps it had already settled too far into the life of moss and reeds.

A NORTHERN HABITAT

    1

My mind is crossed by twisting highland roads.
Across the wilderness of lost generations
(cotton-grass and Flanders poppy flourishing)
it has become a habit not to tempt enemies
or Providence with straight Roman access.

I am not alone in imagining forests returning.

    2

The ghosts sweat, stumble over birch stumps,
exhale midges. In scoured glens there is no room
for all of them and many are again dispossessed.

The emigrants have returned and I am tongueless among foreigners.

    3

Arriving again, I see the moor
like drab tweed. Its gaudy life
survives three inches high.

I measure the old tree
in my mind against the original:
the match is perfect. They repel
each other as stubbornly
as magnets like pole to like.

I rediscover skylines
and cause as little interruption
as twenty, thirty years ago:
heather springs back behind me
yet my feelings twist like strata
in the bedrock above intrusions.

4

Rain glitters between fir trees.
I hold out my hand, it remains dry.

The air is photo-sensitive, alive
with the tracks of migrating particles.

I stand there thinking, an anachronism
lacking the refined senses of an owl.

I move on, leaving my thoughts in the air
behind me, a brief confusion of midges.

5

November in the woods.
I sweat in the wind, rasp
off resinous slabs,
to stack up for winter.

I turn back: my house
is a retreating mirage
and I shall never get near
enough to say "I'm home."

The wind has gone, my breath
inaudible, each
falling flake a maze
of miniature white crosses.

6

The one fir in the garden, stranger
among sycamores, prospers:
a contemporary of mine, now
quite beyond human proportion.

A spire above the arthritic branches
where at the end of autumn we gathered
cold green apples and thought
of summer, its blunt raspberries.

UNDERWATER

1

What happens to the intolerable space?
We stand here at an unmeasured depth
with wine glasses, overshadowed by flowers.
I imagine the surface of the night sky.

"The history of broken things," he says smiling
and I remember the beautiful crystal spheres
that somehow survived the minds dreaming them.
The reflections, the curved fragments, survived also.

"Coming home again," she says, "I watch
the lonely waves unfold in the city streets."
I touch a flower, it tears my hand like coral.
Our words merge as blood whines in our ears.

"La Cathédrale engloutie" next door.
From our own lit windows, dance music
and sudden laughter like glass breaking. We grope
across the lawn like shadows on the ocean floor.

2

What happens to the intolerable weight?
As if flesh became spirit yet was still
flesh, we stand in a giant glass bubble
on the ocean floor. Our ears stop whining.

Instead - "Mahogay Hall Blues" you cry.
I say "Louisss, you blew that note
five years before I was born."
Forty years on and glowing still

(survived like a china cup in an air-raid).

What happens to the intolerable time?
Here it is too deep to flow, it weighs
on the incredibly thin glass of our dream.

"Rapture of the deep": those outside
stare in with distorting faces.
We can see straight through the drained eyes
of those who are forever on the point of dissolving.

3

The history of sunk things. The divers roll
weightless in clear water before descending.
Out of the sun's reach, they will remember
a sphere of intolerable brightness.

Deep enough down in our own element
our element is too much for us, our hearts
race, the music we imagine slows down
as we count survival out by the second.

Bright coral grows on the broken ships.
The all-clear has wailed for a generation.
But down here our ears stop whining
as we yield to the intolerable weight.

"Nitrogen narcosis" of the spirit:
the rainbow shoals, the transparencies
swirl forever before the eye-sockets
through which the darkness on the other side stares.

RAIN
*("There are no sliced divisions. Indian
music is like water."*
                    T.K. Jayaram Iyer)

       1

There is no "tal," all is broken
and where all is broken all
is endless.
We keep hearing the lost music
behind streaming windows, beyond
the trees where rain has the voice
of rivers. There is no "rag" either
so without "tal," without "rag"
the music must be truly lost
and we lost also, ghosts
with dissolving memories.
"The silence beyond silence" - but I
hear each succeeding silence
echo. The wet veils will never close.

       2

It streams down the clear surfaces.
It's the imagination that blurs.
We forget how to talk, listening
to trees, windows.
There is no command yet we obey,
standing more and more still
until our whole existence is
a small dry silence in the rain.

"The silence within silence" -
not a beginning but a dead end.

3

The rain has stopped.
We look through the air clearly
without hearing anything
as if it were thick glass.
There are no words yet to ask
where is the music the rain hid?
The music on the point of being lost
night after night of rain?
When the words come we will not need them.
In the great silence of Becoming
he will greet us familiarly:
his fingers on the sitar string
will no longer remind us of rain.

PASSING THE SOMME

Passing the Somme, gentle green curtains,
the whole countryside is gentle to those
who travel through it with heavy eyelids
mesmerised by shadows racing the train.

Until the train stops, and waits and waits
and no-one leans out and asks why.

In the silence where even the grass-hoppers
among the embankment flowers have been stilled
we stare with diaphanous faces
at the green light slowly rising like a river

until the train, submerged, is insubstantial
and we drift free. Have we been here before?

The green veils part readily.
Our footprints leave no mark
in the white fields where so many ended
in the cramped quarters which are now wide open.

IN MARIEFRED

1

The mists are not quite down on the shorn field.
The ghosts are not yet rustling with old age
but stand around me calmly, apple-trees,
sunflowers, all stooped and ripening still.

Autumn has never haunted me with such wealth
as now: isn't it time to believe the ghosts at last,
my feelings simple as maple leaves going crimson,
my thoughts a generous confusion?

The mists are not quite down on the shorn field
where a reaping machine waits, beyond harvest,
a long neck and jawbone too rigid to stoop.

2

In the silence, in the white light,
yellowing oaks,
the lake still blue and free, no line of vision blocked.
Neither flaw nor darkness in the crystal wall.

My knowledge is acid in the soil,
the weight of fruit pulling to its own decay.
In the silence, in the white light,
a branch of cherries.

My knowledge is too clear.
I look straight through as if it weren't there.

3

Not a ghost but a clear warning:
survival, as the white of a birch bole survives
the rust of autumn.

The mind is a silver landscape: one breath
will mist over a lifetime´s knowledge.
Beyond the clear windows - wastage of seed.

The lanes between the red wooden houses
lead me through both landscapes,
my breath white in the air,

and I too am now one of the ghosts.
We know the warnings - we know, they survive
generation upon generation.

FROM CERTAIN ANGLES

From certain angles a plane coming in to land
looks stationary: I'll return days
later perhaps and it's still there, a fixture.

I remember my grandfather round whom
two generations circled in order.
My own children are circling wider and wider.

I think of this on my way to the post office
with a bundle of airmail letters in my hand:
in a few hours they'll be thousands of miles apart.

IN MEMORIAM ANTONIUS BLOCK

*****

Death: And yet you don't want to die?
Knight: (Antonius Block): Yes. I do.
Death: What are you waiting for?
Knight: I want knowledge.
Death: You want guarantees?
(Ingmar Bergman, THE SEVENTH SEAL)

*****

1

The open spaces are not always open.
In the gloom under the conifers little grows
and the seasons change only the small currency
of nature. Wind in the needles is always the same
and the dry split cones chewed by squirrels
seem ageless. A place for standing still,
perhaps envying trees their roots and toughness,
a place also for endless circular journeys.

At the wood's edge the real nature of the wood
is more easily seen: the dim caves
opening perpetually into each other,
endless choices leading to endless choices,
and above: the dark tufts that hiss in the wind,
the swaying tops. The boles have grown straight
to their predetermined height, you hesitate
among them. To admire you need distance.

Perched like ornaments on dim shelves
owls wait for the bewildering sky to darken.
From the wood's edge you can see the birches
silver and standing at ease before the shadowy

straight ranks. They seem impulsive,
in spring too green, in summer light
each a juggler with a thousand tiny plates
airborne, in autumn rusting ostentatiously.

It has taken you half a lifetime to reach
an understanding with the shadow of the pine.
In the middle of life the dark wood darkens.
You are free to enter or leave, free to measure,
to squander yourself measuring what has no end.
It is a difficult freedom, giving your eyes
half a lifetime to get used to the dark
before they can see the gentle devious rays.

What of the birches? They always stand out
childlike against the dark pines,
their leaves quiver readily, they are full of light
even on dark days, they never brood.
Strange it should take half a lifetime
to watch this fragile game with light
and not once despair, having seen
many closings into darkness.

Coming across snow you stop to look
at a solitary pine pink in the winter sun,
leaning on its blue shadow. There's no white
at all in this white forgetfulness,
your eyes need half a lifetime
to get used to winter light, not to be dazzled
by the glare obliterating familiar shapes
but to acquaint themselves with the devious colours
flowing in black shadows that are never black,
in white fields that are never white.
Their course has no ending.

2

News from a wooded country. To a godlike eye
no two trees are alike, but his eyes
close readily, he dreams of mass-produced trees
and wakens on a white treeless plain, real to him.

Once in a glade he saw the sky for the first time
in years. The white light, blackened in his absence,
burned rings on his mind. He can endure the black
sun only in its pastel reflections beneath the trees.

Once in a glade he saw a dead leaning birch
reflected in a pool so still the reflection
was clearer than the tree itself. His mind's eye
can be too sharp for comfort beneath the trees.

Once in a glade he cut his name on bark, adding
"I am in the middle of life." Now years on
he cut again
"I am in the middle of life still" beneath the trees.

He is walking alone on a white plain. The trees
crowding him in and making his journey difficult
are real enough to him. The white curtains of snow
are real too. At a distance we watch him carefully.

3

The tree, whose green light you praised all
summer, is now
black and infinitely complex against
burnished pale skies.
Hardening in their own time, its branches
are becoming devious, snaky, crooked.

Your imagination has gold borders. You turn

idly page by page
of the giant picture book "The Rise and Fall
of the Tree of Life." The bark wrinkles, rust
beautifies autumn,
each plate shows humanity's
archetypal pose, listening.

Your imagination also has black borders.
Season by season it is never quite untrue
as now you read
"once a man was sitting under a tree."
And the words are true, you're still sitting there
listening, the voice
now is human, neither owl nor
the arthritic creak of wood. Now
the voice rustles, an incessant whispering
"these were our orders, our orders!"

There is no anguish in the voice. You can't reply.
The black borders are a stain spreading inwards.
This picture will soon be a pinpoint.

    4

The great emptiness between Merak and Dubhe
belongs neither to Merak nor to Dubhe.

We are deceived by day. Our eyes shimmer,
widen, cloud over with a blue mist.
We bask under a giant tree, we point
at flowers within reach along the horizon.
We are clairvoyant, hypersensitive:
a pinpoint of light is a distant train
growing smaller and smaller with someone waving
- we forget who it was we parted from.

Towards nightfall our eyes clear.

The blue mist of innocence thins away.
The outer darkness opens. Eyes glint
now peering through screens of foliage
becoming transparent and invisible.
"The outer darkness..." We repeat the phrase
then hesitate as ripple after ripple
widens out. The curves fade and break,
the ripples widen inwards mercilessly.

Merak and Dubhe are pinpoints. They flicker
on a moist light-sensitive membrane.
The great emptiness between them is not theirs.

5

How near. Laced clouds are torn in blue air,
invisible turbulence.
Branches with no leaves have put out flowers.

Spring after spring, they fold into each other,
the old scents that were never old,
still tasting new as the first autumn frost.

You breathe freely, walk through an airy house
with all the doors wide open
expecting to recognise the lost faces and voices.

Year after year, they open out to each other,
the black lines round the edges
melting away, but still not everyone is here,

not everyone finds the invisible doors wide open.
"I still see them large as life."
They are invisible specks on your glass horizon.

How far. The blue air is too clear for comfort.
Thinking a little darkness will help
you close your eyes. Your eyelids are transparent.

6

White, like a magnesium flash
for an early indoor photo. The white
family faces stare in a black mist.

Gold, false spring sun between
one blizzard and the next hurrying after.
Heaven is a blue eye: against such
glaring innocence we wear dark glasses
and keep our thoughts to themselves.

Green, a conspiracy to lull
the restless and keep hidden the white flowers
until they are no longer white and fall.

Gold again. The test for gold is
it will survive acid - this gold
rusts through and through in the bitter air.

"Those are my seasons." His eye is clear,
breaking the white light into a spectrum
whose colours play on us as we count
losses, losing count. How many
in the black mist? in the green? in the gold haze?

He closes his eye on us. We are pale again
as he walks masterfully away, becomes
transparent. We do not envy his gifts.

7

What kind of guilt does he have, likened to
trout lazing and watchful near the still surface,
sides radiant in the occasional filtered gleam,
back dull against waiting buzzard and heron?
His style makes me ask. It paints the buzzard

on glass, balances the true-to-scale heron
on a hair-thin stalk that would snap at a touch.

I ask also because he can change his style at will,
his guilt a pale green stain spreading in the air
(spring at last!), his mind a Winter Palace set,
the crystal gleaming like ice about to melt,
the transparent walls streaming with reflections.
"I shall retire to it when the stale bandages
are unwound: resurrection has a bad smell."

I ask with less and less style: "Guilt for what?"
He replies with more and more: "Think of clouds
piled and luminous on a becalmed ocean." I see
depths full of killed ragged things being eaten;
the predators also need style to clutch at survival.
But what I think, I keep clear of his style. Doubtless
his guilt will survive, still beautiful tomorrow.

    8

Description of a happy era. Why does your black
hand write white words on black
paper? You look up and bare your black
teeth in a smile. The hair you've overdone
(it's too white)
and the trees also
frosted at midsummer by a sun so
black it's almost bursting into colour.

Are there any survivors? You point vaguely
to a corner of white shade and as I approach
I see them: they've made themselves transparent
(ultimate adaptation) and maintain life
of a sort cowering
from the black light.
Those who have been exposed have stained edges,

are nudged constantly away from the purest shade.

Even there, furthest in from the black day
they contend. "Is there no absolute
white, absolute safety?" If there is
it's worth fighting for, ghost eat
ghost. Their teeth rip
black holes in each other.
The torn ones run screaming out in the black
light, become invisible. The victors hunch
closer, more murderous, they are still transparent, still pure.

    9

They have forgotten even their names.
A green flood washes their memories
smooth, all day the sweetness of crushed grass.

"We are at one with antiquity,"
they say, having forgotten everything.
They wake each morning convinced
there was no night.
They listen to voices in the trees,
they yield to temptation.
Some of them smiling stumble
into pools and vanish.

Some of them have been preserved
between the pages of old-fashioned books
and old ladies finger and crumble them
smiling.

A few, a very few, dried
flakes are in safe-deposits
in marble halls supported by everlasting pillars.

10

Pure verticals, pure horizontals, marks
of civilisation. The surfaces are stone-hard,
ground, polished, rigid at beautiful right angles,
an example to the incorrigible curves of nature.

We listen to the incorrigible voices off-stage
prompting, confusing.

Ultimate adaptation: to be transparent,
to stand against the wall and be one with the wall,
an eye without substance yet seeing everything.

"Somewhere in this elegant city there must be
a soft stone, a secret that will yield to the foot,
somewhere in this city a surface must give."

"There is no surface," say the voices of those
whom the surface has long since absorbed.

11

Thick veils of mist pass, reveal,
obscure, reveal, obscure the heavy spire.
I have stopped praying for them to pass
and expose an absolute skyline.
Even if the air stopped perpetually blue
the hunched stones would still turn their backs,
my insistent questions would still flow
smoothly off the round shoulders, vanish
in dim runnels at the depth of the castle walls.
The stones would dry quickly in the clear light
and my eyes, also exposed, would soon darken,
everlasting day become night:
flecks of mica, millions of tiny eyes,
would keep me under surveillance in the shadows.

The space within the thin walls is greater
than the space without. There are long queues
waiting within. They shuffle past slowly,
reveal, obscure, reveal, obscure and mumble...
what do they remember? Why do they ask
such pointed questions and accept such
lying answers? I have stopped praying
for them to reach the front of the line quickly
but I do wish well to those few
who are less vigilant about keeping their places,
who strike a match now and then and see
millions of eye staring in the mist droplets -
those who wish to become pillars of salt
find their wishes granted immediately.

   12

His doubts have divided subtly, they spread
in the air all around him pliable and frail.

The desert where humankind was a thin cloud,
the sheer rock faces - a youthful invention.

In the middle of a dark wood that is neither dark
nor light but a dialectic of shadows,

hesitations, perpetual green rustling,
incessant adaptations to the air.

"But beyond the wood the empty spaces
are waiting to be discovered, between the light
and the dark there are no shadows."

"My roots haven´t budged, I´m standing on them still."

13

"The forest is my natural element. It has
no walls, there is nothing to separate
one fear from another. I pursue my doubt
as it manoeuvres down endless corridors.
The seasons are confident, boles erect, seed
inevitable. Among them I equivocate,
I grope in the light, see my way in denser shadows.
My unease is my knowledge, my confidence."

"The forest was a complex dream you've outgrown.
It's a house of many mansions. All around you
doors you never knew about click shut,
your time is gauged by the quiet closing of doors.
Soon there will be only one window: from it
you will look at a white treeless landscape.
Your white breath on the window will wrinkle
and freeze, in the hard light its ferns will glitter faintly."

from SELECTED POEMS 1963-1978
 (1980)
and FIELDS OF FOCUS
 (1982)

THE CHANGE

"A clean break, that's what you need."
Dry twigs and old ties snap.

I hear the rain, wonder how to count
single drops in the hushed toneless glissandi.

And thinking of all the music I've listened to
how it also has seeped down like the rain,

I imagine an impervious stratum where
it all gathers in a black reservoir

with the power to rise slowly again, a world
barometer keeping its promise of "change."

We'll notice nothing till one morning the fields
reflect the sky, each calm breath

a nuance colouring hundreds of square miles
like a sudden remote key in Beethoven.

PASSING EVENTS

Spring: behind us evenings quietly open,
spaces between houses and trees dilate.

I see an old newspaper in a corner:
it's full of hard facts that have softened
and dried hard again after weeks of change.
It makes a dash across asphalt, flustering
a pigeon, then lies deceptive as a jumping-jack
whose lit fuse seems to have failed.

As the days widen
I walk further just to get home.

IN TOUCH

People set out in the mist. Paris is in a cloud
somewhere, the plane knows. I take a night-train
west through night that's never dark.
Hour after hour of birch-boles in the mist
like the white sticks of a blind population.
A sign with CHARLOTTENBURG is the first
clear message, in letters so huge
only the blind could fail to read them. We cross
an invisible border and the train pauses.
A virtuoso blackbird - he's like
a pianist playing alone in an empty hall.
The forest continues.
My memory has retreated to my fingertips.

OUTLOOK

At last the clear view I've had
all winter is closed.

The trees are no longer ghosts
flaunting their transparency
but now fill out with green
and stand like broad conspirators
between me and what I've seen.

The eye is not merciful.
It reads a face like a sheet of braille
but won't rest there: it sees
always beyond a shoulder
inhuman distances.

I cultivate its weakness,
send it into the wanton traps
of a flowering cherry branch and watch
a world and its after-image blur:
I count out each minute by touch.

MUSEUMS AND JOURNEYS

An exhibition, a century of Edinburgh life.
Coming out I move heavily as a diver
on the ocean floor: one step, one breath
against the weight of the invisible dead. So many
yet the air is clear. And they've no time for me,
their view of the future blocked by giant headlines.

A journey, one I didn't want to take but took,
shutting my eyes, a child again hoping the needle
wouldn't hurt. Lakes and forests, lakes and forests
pass with the weightless ease of delirium. So many.
My view of the past stays clear but hard to read
like a radio-map of a secret corner in the night sky.

Museums and journeys. We meet as strangers do
at the end of long ellipses over continents.
We exchange histories, our view of the present clear
but the landscapes go on sliding past. So many
memories, I try to say "One at a time!"
They keep piling up like urgent unanswered letters.

VISINGSÖ

Gustavssons and Johanssons laid in packed rows:
each grave is a black hole in space.
The eye sees grass, the mind teeters
like a child trying to cross a stream on stones.

(I remember a building with big mirror windows,
the blue and yellow summer shone back at us.
The people inside could have been dead
could have been watching us in pity or envy.)

The white boats never seem to get bored
repeating the same trip. They'll fade from photos.
Like a blind man I hold on to railings
and the bright water hurts when I stare at it.

They say it's deep. There's no harm in agreeing
as my mind gropes for the next wet stepping-stone.

MIDSUMMER NIGHTS

Past midnight, the sky already white:
soft clouds can't stop, pines
sway from the waist, aspens hiss.
My house when I reach it stares at me
with the pallor of someone close to death.
I must sleep, I fumble with dark blinds,
imagine the walls going transparent,
mutter "if only the mirrors could be black."

RUNMARÖ

An ice-age boulder, gross
solitary of the forest.
A boat in the grass, roped
in black plasic, for committal.
A collapsed smithy, the bellows
the hard-worked lung.

These survive while the forest
quietly absorbs its own,
generations of mushrooms
and "Swedish soldier" flowers,
houses awash to the eaves
and Baltic family histories.

A photo: we´re green and brown
in a brown and green world.
We´re speechless, half-open-
mouthed for air. A radio
sits on a bright table,
an ice-age marvel on display.

REVELATIONS

Like a huge eye: an intolerable flash
of pure vision, then a roar of pain.
A whole day's light compressed in a second

and the landscape "as it really is" - leaves
in X-ray, animals' brains at ebb,
our skulls nestling in haloes of imagination.

In light or dark, for us the clichés are real:
the hair I don't have on my spine rises,
at the window the dead faces jump into life.

The TV at least is blank, switched off.
All evening it was a cool polyglot.
The dead and the living faces stared through me

even the frantic woman on the smuggled film
blackening and flashing because of the "bad conditions"
as she listed her husband's sufferings "under treatment,"

the banal delirium of facts "as they really are",
fact upon fact, her Russian so feverish
the Swedish subtitles could hardly keep up.

I count seconds. Continuous replay.
The first crackle of rain is the sudden clattering
of a terrified crowd in a narrow street.

A TREE ALONE

I set out alone, came back alone, and the tree
had spent all day standing alone in the mist.
(The haze cleared once and I saw a horse
that may have been dead, may have been sleeping.)

Late into the night I spelt my way like a child
through proof-sheets of old poems, my red
marks warning: "Deceased, Not To Be Disturbed."
I'm still there, promisingly alive, although
the moment I recognise me I keep turning away
into a future I can scarcely expect me to know.

Moonlight. Clarity at last. The tree gleams by itself.
I feel secure making certain he's still there.
By the look in his eyes, if he had eyes,
he wouldn't seem to know I'm here.

REMEMBERING AN ISLAND

"Island
what shall I say of you, your peat-bogs.
your lochs, your moors and berries?" Strange words
to recall on a Stockholm street-crossing, it's like
a dream where you find a door in a solid wall.

North-east, east and south-east
a top-heavy pile of thunderclouds,
west over Kungsholmen a glassy fire:
between, the city is a Dutch masterpiece,
still-life with evening traffic-flow.

And not a dream. I know where the walls end
and begin again. I touch doors on time.
The Highland roads in my mind have been redeveloped -
a few old curves still visible, like the creases
in my birth-certificate from the thirties.

NIGHT-MUSIC

I listen to music I haven't heard for fifteen years
and remember every note. As if a conversation
paused for a moment which became a lifetime
and no-one noticed. In such familiarity
across years which of us two is stranger?
My 1959? My 1974?
I can't tell who asks, who refuses to reply.

I wear head-phones. In the black window I see
a man wearing equipment for a brain operation.
It seems to work. Each half of my head slowly
rediscovers the lost art of independence.
And other losses too, when I take them off:
silence to the right, silence to the left, I hear both
knowing now there is no way of turning my back.

Morning. First snow. Silence from fields and woods.
I feel warm in it, though the music is coiled
away in silence, though each word said is muffled
by the soft ghost of silence clinging to it. The winter
sun is late yet the room is full of a pale light
as if news had just come of someone's death
and no-one has begun asking questions, and no-one answers.

A FIFTEENTH CENTURY TRIPTYCH

JOHANNES OCKEGHEIM

A Scandinavian Airlines DC9
whines over in the mist, courting the one
chance in millions, touching earth on time.
There's no danger in looking at the sun today,
it's white like a new coin. In the silence
I press a switch - no not a ghost

but fear and recognition across five
centuries. You cry out against
the black lake, "obscura tenebrarum."
A space where even electricity fails.
Last night I dreamt of cancer in the thigh
and the terror of an absent-minded surgeon's knife.

HIERONYMUS BOSCH

The screen crackles. A Camdodian family
still-life: caught in a shell-blast.
The damned always outnumber the saved.
Nothing moves, the camera's rock-steady.
Hell is all surface, torture by colour,
an eternity of eyes that can't close.

A marvellous statement of the obvious
is what you painted, knowing the ocean depth,
like the subconscious, is all law and order.
I press a switch and the screen is blank again.
I still have pre-electric dreams.
I am a wooden saint tortured by cracks.

ROBERT HENRYSON

"Sub specie aeternitatis,"
a reading lamp like a prison searchlight.
Humanity feeling its way along a wall.
Inside of hell? Outside of heaven?
Your universe has a double tongue, speaking
of the winter behind a sweating judge's brow.

"Rycht marvelous a mekle multitude" -
the mare, the swallow, the solitary saved,
true outsiders. A hand from the dark
swivels the light in my eyes: confess! confess!
I waken. The light's been on all night.
Now in the morning it hardly reaches the page.

THE WAITING ROOM

I wait, thinking of a rowing-boat I saw
at rest on transparent water, not
quite at rest, testing its rope, resting
the weight that kept it steady and weightless.

Something from Beethoven goes on and on
at the side of my mind, a bad-tempered neighbour.
Strange how so much impatience
won through to such inhuman calm.

I wait. A fan drones. It's so
monotonous the room could be in flight.
I stare at a mirror. All it shows
is the reflection of a pale barred window.

TRAVELLING NORTH IN SPRING

A place whose name means "middle of the wood."
Then a town Germans once razed.
And on. Each place, distorting like
the notes of the crossing-bells, lets us through.

Things take their revenge on the naked eye.
White birches, yellow wooden houses
incandesce. I close my eyes - the snow
burns through, someone's demanding an answer.
I try to concentrate on a basking log
forgotten with a mile of blue water to itself.
No use. It's past. Lean torrents
explode down unscaleable cliffs.

Spring gets later. At journey's end I try
to imagine dark woods. I find myself
looking up at a saint with a sword in his hand.
The pavement gives more light than it receives.

TRAVELLING ALONE

The countless forests we pass hour after hour,
they are anonymous with such grace.
Would we feel safer
if all the dead came back and stood waiting?

The north train and the south train pass.
Sitting in one I see myself in the other.
Without much grace
I keep crossing my own invisible path.

A film suddenly stopping in a crowd scene:
black holes in space, where the people were.
Each has stepped into
the outer darkness of his own company.

THINGS THAT LAST

At night I go astray in the expanding universe.
I fall into a black hole in my head,
panic briefly at the idea of anti-sleep.

In the morning I visit a farmstead museum.
Wooden utensils that wore lives away
lie heaped like the clothes of a missing person.

They seem bigger and heavier than the tiny events
that need millions of miles of elbow-room,
whose voices need light-years to reach us.

Smooth handles are covered with vague scratches:
from certain angles they look as meaningless
as the pen-marks on Beethoven's manuscripts.

READING LAGERKVIST ON THE DAY HE DIED

A lifetime ago he walked away
alone from the circus tent. Under the stars
he weighed his doubt and found it was too light.
"What do I know that gives me the right to doubt?
What do I believe that gives me the right to deny?"

I follow the forest roads mile after mile
darkening into a night that never darkens.
In the white nights there's always a black hour.
Something in my mind goes pale like a birch
among pines caught in a quick breeze.

Head packed with catastrophes. Into
the woods. Supernatural footfalls.
I stop in a wide clearing, the trees ranged
back like a breathless crowd waiting to see
what sort of fight I make with silence.

All the bright day the shadows move
round: simple cause, obscure effect.
Almost dark here, and I feel almost
anonymous - but for this aspen,
a single white leaf, a frantic pendulum.

WAKING IN THE SMALL HOURS

After such dreams, to land just here.

Half asleep, I count defences. First, the sea
round the island. Then the forest round the house.
Then the house round me. I lie thinking
of forest paths, doors opening and closing.

Half awake, I pull aside the curtain and look
up: white sky. Black forest edge.
Up and up. I think of the piled constellations.
It feels like leaning over the edge of a high tower.

Reality, so plain and inescapable.
I leave it again without noticing I´m going.

HOME THOUGHTS

If I were to return now after
"an absence?" But while absent I have gained
too much presence. It's where I live.

I add years, change houses, keep
track of myself. I post letters to the past
and answers come, always up to date.

The generations are always catching up.
The tall historic houses will still be leaning
forward like runners waiting for the starting-gun.

It's dusk - but for a pin-hole in the clouds:
a ray of sunlight glares on an empty field.
Something I can't see is being interrogated.

LISTENING TO RACHMANINOV IN A NEW HOUSE

A storm on the building site. It´s un-shipshape,
plastic sheeting in a frenzy to shred itself free.
And outside my window raw pale boulders
clawed up - from how many dark ages?

But each roof is tested, settles to holding fast.
I fingerprint fresh timber, like touching a branch
far inside a forest; anonymous perhaps
yet the memory cells in my fingertips keep it.

So much space in the present. My letters travel,
solitary migrating birds, they find the address,
but small spaces between words can be so wide
years can slip through, ring after ring in the tree.

A resinous house then with no smell of the past.
The dead wood will live through generations
not mine. At night I listen to the forest in my head
and christen the new house with music written in exile.

STOPPING BY SHADOWS

High up, birches have a homely aspect,
small, like things we discover and recognise
returning after an absence of many years.
They're almost transparent in the snow
and above, boulders as big as cathedrals
poise, on the edge since prehistory.

Midday. I stop at the edge of the shadow
that has filled this space all winter,
the sun a white breath at the cliff-top,
a brief flame in the ice of a remote tree.
I watch my own shadow dissolving
slowly in the luminous dark air

then take a cold step back to life,
skis hiss-hissing on snow-crystals
that spent all night quietly hardening.
Across the valley red and yellow figures
on a brilliant field jump into focus
like true events under a microscope.

RESOLUTIONS

All day the air got harder and harder.
I woke in the small hours, rooftops

frozen seas of tranquility, while far
below the first flakes fell on the street.

The air of another planet come down to earth,
we breathe harshly between familiar stones.

No place for flesh. Spirit and bone
at odds, the nerves caught between, singing:

"Must it be?" It must be must be must be
bouncing like a ball in a small room without windows.

AFTER A JOURNEY TO A NEW FOUND LAND

Hundreds of small hard knocks at the window.
All the dreams stop waving their arms,
collapse like seaweed left by the tide.

Yesterday I came to the end of a journey,
like a nomad unpacked memories,
settled the bare rock with private trees.

The day before, I pretended there was no journey,
fumbled at the telephone dial, each voice
felt at my fingertips like braille.

Today, silence, like the noise of early rain
on leaves. The sun touches stones and they give
the remote smile we see on the faces of the blind.

MUSIC AND FLIGHT

Rachmaninov in flannels at Locust Point:
old photos just stare back.
Music's different. Through my headphones
I hear him playing in 1924,
the rustle of time, fifty years of mist,
the piano in a small room next door,
but still the dead hands reach me true.
Would it have chilled him to know I'd listen in ?

Music and flight. Above the cloud-cover
in a blue world with a huge curve at the edge
we never reach, there's nothing to hold onto.
Illusions vary - my hands hold each other.
Be still, keep moving fast or fall.
I think of the brain-cells that store music,
glittering in silence, waiting. I look down,
the space below me deep as fifty years.

Between flights I haunt forests and cities,
packed places full of rooms and clearings.
The great secret doors that open quietly
and close behind us once or twice in a life,
we learn to live with, they take their time.
The older I grow the more space I find
behind the small doors I touch by chance,
they always open, nature contradicted:

the world becoming denser as it expands.

BIRTHDAYS

You want to hide. You say it's like
a taxi ride in a foreign city,
when'll it end? - panic and price
and blood-pressure and a lost address.

Perhaps. I think of forests,
an apparition not stark
but like the slow freshening
of a birch among dark surrounding conifers.

COMING BACK

I forget the sea, passing the first
lighthouse after a voyage.
I drive home through forests,
darkness rising between pines.

New memories fold for the night.
The forest goes on growing in the dark
where I lie thinking of the slow rings
behind me, around me, before me.

LIGHT FROM THE NORTH

My watch could well be a century out.
I walk past birch-boles, they're pale
like the dark side of the moon clear at last.

My hand rests on a smoothed pine plank
whose years flow like thin lines of water
from a calm boat. The forest is best

now, wide day at dead of night,
I feel like someone wakened from an illness
still knowing how far he's been.

I look towards morning but it's yet
white and cold like the lake through trees.
I wait for sleep, as horizontal as I can.

SOMETHING LIKE A SKY

Something in us has suddenly cleared.
Like a sky.
Like a still-life, alive.
Behind us, our footsteps and voices.
Behind the walls, a wide silence.
The air is white and open, ready for snow.

ANCIENT TIMBER

The roof restored in the 1490s... carved
bears still clutching their staffs, power
we admire briefly, preferring to pause longer
by old houses that have spent centuries
twisting into the shape of trees again.
Something in the dead wood refuses to die.

Night. On the way home we briefly admire
a giant constellation atilt and faint
above cherry blossom like carved stone.
Given time (more than we've got)
we could watch The Great Bear dissolve.
Given time, nothing constellates.

But we do, for a time. Our rich hours
lightly weigh into our instant past.
We can hold each other round the clock
and still ask: is skin-deep deep?
Beyond touch, where do we find each other?
Something between us refuses to let go.

SAFE MORNINGS

Dreams get deeper and colder, like sea-water.
No end, it seems, to the world that tilts away
from the swimmer's feet, shadows of departure
widening between us like the hulls of wrecks.
No end to it, it's here and now and true,
it's our own element we're drowning in,
each lost in the dream of losing each other.

Morning. As if I climb out of the water, white
and under-exposed, and lie down on a wooden jetty.
For hours the boards have soaked up the early sun,
for years gathered warmth even on dull days,
the dead wood is still alive as I breathe
resin and my breath fills out minutes
to hours and I imperceptibly darken.

SOMETHING WE DIDN'T KNOW WAS THERE

Goldfish in the reflection of bricks.
Steep buildings round us, barely a glimpse
of English perspectives beyond,
moderate hills, moderate groups of trees,
the buildings murmur like transformers,
all the words we don't hear, the eyes
we don't see, the work we're not doing.

Awake, I start dreaming. Landscapes
small and distant, close-by and large,
grow dull. We could be trapped in a faded
photograph a hundred years old,
figures beyond remembrance or pity,
less recognisable than things,
ageless grass seeding in clear focus.

Dreams chill. And sounds. In the quiet
bushes sparrows are chirping louder and louder.
The pond wrinkles and grows young again
and wrinkles. We shiver at last and look up -
eclipse! A black hole where the sun should be.
We believe what we see, we believe
extremes when we see them and hurriedly gather

books coats, ask "Are you cold?"

IN MEMORIAM. AGAIN

His books still weigh the same on my shelf
but suddenly look at me like strangers.
I stare back at his smile in the newspaper,
the black dots distant as The Milky Way.

Thinking this, I don't hear the rain
start - hard to believe the sound of rain
after a dried-up summer. I rush
out, it's true, dead leaves are wet,

dust smells of fresh-turned earth.
I watch the new rain make rings
on the black lake, try to count but can't.
They overlap like the words in a crowded room.

HOT DAYS IN CAMBRIDGE

"King's Closed." No chance to see
stone mimicking air. No matter -
the act will still be there lives from now.

Instead, we row in circles on heavy water
and ask how many pages are in a tree
and trudge round on deserts that were lawns

and lisen to the languages of Europe
strain and wilt, tired defenceless wings.
We all wait for evening, evening comes

bringing Haydn's "Creation" on the radio,
music from an unheard-of future
when these stones were sweated into place.

Our bodies radiate, they're winter stoves.
All night beside an open window
cool air is iron on my wet back.

NIGHT ALONE

Friends, you walk away beneath trees
you've known since childhood. On dark earth
you walk like brief gentle visitors.
We call goodnight earnestly as if
morning will be another continent
and none of us will know the word for "morning."

One of me, the one who talks and waves,
turns a switch and lets the darkness in
and falls asleep at ease in the forest silence.
The forest is never silent. The other me,
the stubborn one who never talks and can't
lies awake as always listening listening

to sounds behind sounds as night opens
outwards and down. How deep and far
does silence lie? Nothing there to stare
out. He gropes, switches music on,
music that falls like light across his body,
that continent without words for anything.

NOTES FOR A SUMMER

"The Seasons" we can always play again.
Our summer's ended, new prints
we can copy and send, copy and send.
Outside: leaves dead from drought.
Inside: music imitating rain.

"Our" summer? We passed a graveyard
and I thought of heavy stacked photo-plates,
pictures waiting undeveloped, water
and calm trees invisible and black.
Tomorrow grows wider and wider, waiting.

Vivaldi clicks off. Silence. Back
to spring again? No. Sleep. And the first
few slow inches of a long journey.

TRAVELLING

Islands crawl across the wet windows.
They swell, undulate in slow motion,
shrivel astern, keep looming past
as sky and water blacken into night.

We step ashore, keeping our own size
while the boat-lights shrink and disappear
and the island grows wide around us.
We breathe raw earth and potato haulms.

We draw blinds. The room's secure now.
It's bigger than the island. And the wind
so loud and near in withered rowans
still keeps a certain quiet distance

as we spread worn maps under the lamp
and remind each other of where we've been.
At last, behind closed eyelids
nothing holds us in, we drift out.

Next morning I look down from a plane
on glittering blue water, punctual boats
on tiny endless voyages to and fro
between placid immovable islands.

MARAZION

The Mount - it's so familiar I don't
even say "There it is at last."
It is. A postcard true to life.

We're out of season so the beach is bare,
only dunlins, oyster-catchers, sandpipers
picking over dull hanks of weed.
The tide has turned. We could wait and walk
right over, touch it. But don't.

It's how we see our other lives, the ones
we didn't, can't live. We recognise,
move on, know they're still there.

ELEGIES

The hotel room is cramped, with five
very unequal sides.
First snow shrinks, grey ordered heaps,
last leaves are lemon-bright.
That's Oslo, that's today,
cool oaks and warm stones
we leant against yesterday.
How uncertain, like things
once read about in Mandeville.

I dream of Tresco, raw
mist unravelling through
un-English palms. We lost our way
on a small well-mapped island.
That was true. Waking I add:
through a bright chasm
the helicopter pounced at last.
If seeing's believing I have that
summer stacked on photographs.

I dream again, trapped in
rigid staves of impossible music.
I don't see but have to believe
until back in my narrow room.
I wait for all those moments
to settle.
I think of gentle animals at ease,
not minding our presence, not
seeming to notice our absence.

PLACES TO STAY IN

1

"Not home but where I stay."
Some places force you to stay.
It's like stepping off a train
halfway through a journey
and being left. Or being given
a new outlandish name
and told it's yours now, for ever.

2

A well-known café, ablaze
with heart-felt light. But look:
people are less than life-size
and half the more than life-size
tables are empty. Across blue
unwarmed cobble-stones
late homecomers darken.

3

Nine rooms empty at last.
Their furniture fills my mind
and always will. Not that being
happy or not tells, rather
a fair lifetime spent.
The garden has been seen to by one
summer's workmanlike weeds.

4

He's stuck, we said. The place
is too small. He's gone dull
brooding on his predicament

of being local. He ought to move.
He didn't. And here he is now
surprising us with brightness,
mortality with a new face.

THE MANSE

I see again the vexed garden trees
still green and tossed
so long ago I panic
to think the person watching them is me.

Hear again icy arguments
in a winter chimney,
flung distorted quarter-hours
from the unfailing war-memorial clock.

I come now, feeling too modern
in my present tense,
embarrassed behind my camera,
trying to catch something, before what?

Twenty-eight years of keeping the weeds
down undone
by one summer's harsh growth.
Knots of twine still hang from wires.

Doors that opened closed, opened closed,
opened closed, opened…
Draughts have their way at last
across acres of unfurnished floor.

The picture I take is of the present tense
only. Only the house.
Grey. And trees I grew with,
watched cold sunsets through.

An inhospitable image
but a true one.
The walls look damp as they wait
for a next generation of set fires.

TURNING FORTY

Insects live in tree-high grass.
I hardly see the grass, look up
at tree-high trees. Birds touch
down on their swaying terra firma.
It's all perspective, I know, I know.

Most humans are dead. Books, music,
thoughts, gadgets, most buildings even,
work of dead hands. We don't own
much. "Today" keeps circling the earth,
lighting the tips of sullen icebergs.

Clearest things are seen from the side.
Boarding a ship, a green depth glimpsed.
Or coming out of sleep, two worlds
transparent, shining through each other
a slow second, and one goes dark.

Perspective changes, down hill and up
hard to distinguish, deepest change
prepared when least expected.
I don't recognise the forty-year-old
hurrying past me, the opposite way.

KEEPING STEADY

Water-borne I watch the boat's shadow
flow over lichen-covered rock,
shadow on shadow as if the lichen
too were on its slow way past.

Air-borne I watch mottled islands
drift with the ease of clouds. I've left
days of my life on one of them and now
I carry the island, an invisible weight.

On land again, still seeing the curved
earth I lean to stay upright
then settle my newest memories
on an old point of balance. It's like the pause
clock-hands make at midnight.

WHAT TO DO WITH THE WORD "HOME"?

I handle it like an antique-
collector (though I'm none)
back with a prize, unique to him
but heavy, heavier as he stands
at a loss where to set it down.

Would it suit here? Would eight
years of youth qualify?
Bog-myrtle and peewit,
curlew and cotton-grass
are sweet ghosts but don't claim
special attention and don't get it.

The moor's ambiguous. I've no
talent or desire to join
an inch of life lying low
over the spongiest, most
patient of collectors. It is
experienced in swallowing homes.

Can I settle here only
on first arrival, in my pocket
a ticket for the clear sky?
The people who still live here -
they've been moving as fast as I.

A NIGHT AND A MORNING

Passing the cathedral spire
I see two clock-faces,
one bright, one blank.
How many bricks,
used-up muscles, time
kept like a cold monument.

The library walls are black.
Light from a hurrying half-moon
glints on them like seawater.
How many books,
used-up voices, pages
unreadable in the dark.

Almost asleep I turn and see
through a thin drawn curtain
shining windows and street-lamps
the height and depth of the hillside.
They're a dense constellation
less than a hundred years old.

Almost awake again, I think
the white spring light is snow
on roofs and streets. It's not. I try
to focus on an unfamiliar day,
all the dead ones at my back
crowding to watch the new one.

FLYING OVER ARRAN

Fields I got lost in.
I retched on the raw smells beneath
imperfect grain, dreamt
of cornflowers filling the sky.

In dreams I've commuted there,
always on time, shaking
off travellers' jinxes,
opening doors, turning corners -
as if a sun-warmed stone
had kept warm for forty years.

Passing where I was born
four decades later and
thirty thousand feet higher,
New World sweat in my pores,
was not what I expected.
Pale micro-fields in a haze:
I take a picture down through space.
Only an outline shows.
Something light-years away,
a blow-up, cupped in my hand.

EAST COAST REVISITED

Jonshaven, that was three years.
Edinburgh, that was thirteen.
Holy Isle, that was two visits
with fifteen years between them.

Is this being god-like, observing
autobiography at a safe height?
The cabin is full of sun; sensations
from earth are folded in newspapers.

Less god-like to chafe against
horizons crowding me in;
to wear my watch all night,
faint substitute for a fixed star.

FROM 1939

What quick hands the dead have, and eyes
more metallic than a blackbird's.
I'm alive, but slow, and so much
has happened since, I listen to him play
through a noise like early rain on leaves.

ON AN ETCHING OF DEDHAM VALE
 By Glynn Thomas

A rural "mappamundi," stream and stile,
random English fields become a world
in a fish-eye lens, and at the centre
convolvulus and poppy, man-size.

A world to carry through the world, a check
on the eye's life-long growing pains.
Lesson One: "Take your time!"
Lesson Two: "Your time's running out!"

Time I spend in "Dedham Vale" is time
that waits, with interest, behind the glass.

UNDATED PHOTOGRAPH

The dead had the whole world to themselves then.
Brahms leans, uncomfortably
close to tipping over, less kempt
than the tied leafless creeper on the wall.
He looks at me as if I weren't there.
He must have stared at me a moment before
getting up and finishing his life.

In his own good time of course. It's this
photo that hurried off through space,
eighty years later? reaching me
like today's news. And on. News that'll still
be news in the twenty-first century.
Like a generous miracle it leaves
a fair copy of itself in my brain.

In silence. What of the black notes lying
untidy as seeds in closed pages,
in the dark where no-one can read
or hear them? All they can do is wait.
I think of arctic lupin seeds once
found after ten thousand years
in ice - unabashed, they rooted and flowered.

That's extreme. Someone must be playing
Brahms somewhere, always, another extreme,
his music a rare element in the air.
Look, his hands are stiff as dead wood.
Look, as the ash fell from his cigar
and invisible preparations were made
for a new season's crowding weeds.

FOLLOWING A MIRROR

I look past a stranger's eye and see,
out through an open door, a line
of leafless birches like blind men
leading west. The mirror can't stop:
an ocean, white ruins of icebergs,
a prairie, parallels converging,
a desert, towns with pale street-grids
and invisible houses, El Paso
down through the hazed skyline.
The mirror keeps everything I lose.
I sleep. The mirror stays awake in the dark.
The stranger's eyes are shut. The mirror hurries
surefooted on narrow cliff paths,
its memory for local history
immaculate, how to find houses -
one of Caithness flags with a deep press
stacked with nineteenth century boxes;
a manse in Arran, prewar rain
smudging garden trees; last year's
hotel room, a slit view of the Cam.
And all crowded. People I forgot
and those I remember exchange faces.
Sharp details swell like thunder clouds,
meeting rooms grow miniscule.
Trapped in a rib-cage, I stop breathing
gasp at the last moment, break into
morning - morning, a place I didn't choose,
a wide hall where I wait for baggage
while out on wet tarmac behind me
engines that have droned all night cool.

LOSS OF OUTLOOK

Easter. Days with no workmen
hammering up moulds, pouring soft
concrete, waiting, undoing wood.
No walls will rise today. Old snow
rots to a clockwork drip round
the clock from half-finished thresholds.
Through wet glass I watch high
wet gallows lean in the east wind.

I think of midwinter when I watched
fresh snow pile on timber stacked
beside a measured square cut in rock.
My westward view of trees was still clear.
And five wrens went bounce bounce
between piled stack and piled eave
while a red sun went right down
and wouldn't come again for eighteen hours.

By midsummer my view will be gone.
So will the tall crane whose double chain
sways all night with empty hands.
On other sites windows will come for those
about to acquire newer and higher views
than the one I thought worth keeping.
I'll see a wall beyond which light
clouds and planes with rows of people fly.

EDGES

No head for heights, and life is high.
Like you, I have to allow myself the odd
moment of trust, like the high-wire walker
looking up and letting his foot find the wire.

The next bold step is spring. I watch
a new caterpillar on a new leaf -
he tests the buoyant tip and turns back.
Nothing between leaf edge and nearest cloud.

"The Art of Fugue" ends like a broken arch.
From high-wire to ground, a hundred feet.
From leaf to cloud, a hurrying mile.
Nothing between the last quaver and us.

HURRYING IN SPRING

An ambulance draws a fast white line,
wails in discordance. Inside a head stoops.
Avenue pines have grey undersides.
Rude spirals of dust dervish at crossing-places.
Spring is nervous, or I am. I stride
on a moving walkway, walls rushing with ease.
Calm days I remember all shake,
slip, their vertical hold awry.
Something in me's a compass-needle that knows
where north is but can't, for trembling, rest and point.

PASSING VERDUN

Some things ought to be looked at.
I'm driving east from Rheims. The closer I get
the tighter the motorway's grip on me.
Signs I've waited for point, I can't
obey, I'm on rails, I'm carried past

cross a border, turn north, stop
at a house with thick walls and echoing rooms.
I wind my watch back and gain an hour.
I have a view of Cassiopeia, stars
so slow they were once called fixed.

Headlights float in pairs round
a wood-edge, short-lived as moths.

NOTE FOR A JAPANESE POET

"Hitomaro." Something lands softly
on the net of my feelings. At first I don't
think of thirteen centuries,
our instant panic if we met. "I can't..."
is what we'd each say, fail to say,

forgetting to look up at the twisting elms
that had already made him make sense to me.

LISTENING TO A CURLEW

1

A perpetual silence at my side.
Everything I hear leans
towards it, like trees stooped
by a lifetime's coastal wind.
Or in the deep rock beneath
our feet seams rise and dip
we'll never see. Or at a play
we step on layers we didn't know
were there, they give, they hold, they give,
and after the last words hands
try to clap the silence away.

2

Me, under a saguaro.
Next, you, instead of me.
We prove what we can - "July
-77, Arizona."
Count woodpecker holes
but not a wing whirrs. Stare
at the thundercloud about to pour
boulders across the desert road.
We couldn't see the next hours
we've now lost. We couldn't hear
this silence that we've saved.

3

We always know what came next.
Listening to the prelude
we always hear the silent fugue.
What comes next - each hour
I follow the glass wall between

the good silence and the bad.
On which side? What will I hear?
On this side I say thanks
be to silences that let,
say, a brief curlew's
voice ring year after year.

FINDS, circa 1948

Lupins. Father-figures, I reached up
and rolled a ball of dew from a green hand.

Calendulas. They made widows older,
curtains paler, afternoons heavier.

Harebells on crumbling grassy cliffs.
My fear of edges became lifelong.

Wild nasturtiums by a pool deeper
than places of silence and perpetual night.

A PHOTO, A CLOCK

"May." The year I forgot to write.
The hands say ten thirty-three.
They've said so for decades perhaps.
Long enough, in this red and green
preserved clock-maker's house. Round
the giant dial thirty-two points
make it a sun, a cogged wheel in some
heavenly device. And you paused
a nervous five-hundredth of a second,
clear as frost
beside a stopped clock whose hands are blurred
and watery beyond your field of focus.

REVISITING A CLOCK

September rushed. It stopped only when we
stopped, again, in front of the stopped clock.
That fits. This is the "old" town,
a genuine dead street in dead Aarhus.
Through-traffic for visitors: at night
any visitants will not be seen.
I take another picture but the glass
between me and the burnished spiked dial
is too alive,
thronged with eager shadows. Back to the car
we say, with cold hands, follow
follow the scurrying white backs of leaves.

READING A PAGE

I stare at a well-made page. Words
that will never break ranks wait
for me. I hardly reach the first stop,
turning and turning to the window to watch
a generation of snow in thin air,
fluff, soon ragged discs,
mass obedience to one law,
identical souls, homonyms.
The snow-flakes throng in. The whiter
the light gets the less there is to see.

The page is black, the words an icicle.
I blow on it, it melts, it melts not,
and someone says: "This is your page,
you have only one, birth at the top,
death on the bottom line. Each day
survived means more to miss out,
the summary becomes denser, clear truth
defying nature, clearer as it thickens."
My completed decades begin
to glow with their own concentration.

REMEMBERING WALLS

I once wanted these walls
to turn magically clear
as air and let me walk through.

Now that strangers have moved in
strange furniture I want
the house to be solid and dour,

resisting the dank strath winds
and to the dry pine-descant
adding a worn ground-bass

angular, melancholy.
It follows me from winter to
winter. Safe in its lulls

voices that cannot last long,
that did not always please me,
will last as long as I will.

No-one watches the wet slates
dry and glisten again and dry.
My private music remembers me.

WALKING IN WOODS

Trees with the patience of sleep-walkers
who've stopped and forget to move on.
Woods have their own gradual timetables.

I move too quickly to catch more
than forest trivia, patiently years
creak, not a hint of a Great Plan.

In part of the timetable I can't see
trees waken and move to the next stance.
They need space, passing circumspectly.

I come home knowing little as ever.
Resin wears off. I almost hear
a music so slow it can't be heard.

from COMING DOWN TO EARTH
AND SPRING IS SOON
(1990)

ARRIVING BY TRAIN, DECEMBER

Less familiar miles are quick.
Further north, each mile
thickens and slows. Gorse, rowan,
pine, without seeing them
I recognise the way they lean.

A croft light, one more.
I fill the black space between
with names like Lothbeag or Loth
(public policies) and quick
unstoppable recall:

instants of weather, the bend
of reeds, campions under larch
I know are felled, a raised beach
whose stones never seemed to warm.
Private policies, no doubt.

Father's waiting shape watches
five strangers alight, one
of whom stops and becomes me.
Our feet make the same sound
creaking home on new snow.

THE SWING BRIDGE

The bridge holds because it gives way.
Grey wires, planks weathered white
give to father's tread, which I try to match.
Crossing alone is worse: my careful step
goes spongy, almost walking-on-air.
And the wet air is loud; even in June
the fresh and hectic water never stops.

Last time I came to find the bridge,
a decade ago, there was none.
Must've been quick, I thought, to roll it up
and bundle it off. Its grace was flimsy.
Yet how much space is left, as if
a crowded tenement had been cleared.
And how my feet remember its queasy sway.

RAILWAY EMBANKMENTS

1

The life of railway embankments,
mostly a life passed, except
when a train stops and waits and waits

and no-one speaks or leans out
into the solid foreign landscape
bigger than life. "Still Life

with Russell Lupin and Active Bee."
And its own timetable. In time
it could well take us in, moss

having a quiet but steely claim
on wheels that have lost the will to turn.
We wait, exhibits from another age.

2

The life of railway embankments,
private, like dreams we pass
night after night but can't touch.

The life of willow-herb, rust,
hot stones. Father said
"Walk on the sleepers not the ash."

The step was too short for him.
Too long for me. The tips
of our fishing-rods bounced at odds.

HOME GROUND

I leave a long journey behind. An old sense
of gravity returns as I watch experts
dismantle a house. Rafters, in daylight again,
are stacked to one side like casualties.

I count years on the spot. Climb on the level.
Perhaps
I'm a diver on the ocean floor outstaying my time.

ALIVE AGAIN

I revisit.
All in place, bare hill (not
to be moved), dying crofts (still dying),
manse garden tangled, in disgrace.
I forgot
how loud the past can be. The wind
(the strath's oldest inhabitant) still tugs
awry the megaphone cries of rooks,
ruffles
the harsh quarters of the war-memorial clock.
Time beats against a current, can't
always be counted on to hold its own.

ALMOST A HABIT

Loch Araichlin - I almost reach you.
Peaty rills keep you full. They bring
endless gossip from miles around
of low life (inches high) and vast
leisured cloud-shadows. You take it all
into your monosyllabic lap-lapping -
except that on quiet nights you hush

all you have received into a silence
I heard once and can't stop hearing.
I drive up the strath and stop and wait
by Loch An Ruathair, look past the loch
I see and hear towards the one I can't.
Almost a habit, after thirty years,
visiting a loch I never try to see.

ON NOT SAYING MUCH

I drive past forests with so many shades
of green I ask, could any language list them?
Their light touches me from a time before words.

Their light makes me want to say no to things
that demand allegiance, to say yes to things
that never demand allegiance but deserve it.

I reach a friend's house: veranda railings,
neighbour's car, they have the look of heirlooms
untouched in attics. The thick dust is pollen.

SHOSTAKOVITCH Opus 138

Ripe rowan-berries tight to the point of bursting
grossly overcrowd a slender branch at my window.
What I hear is less of a harvest song than a lament
climbing and dying in semitones, frozen steppes,
black on white, wide between narrow rainbow notes,
and a weight of knowledge and sorrow,
"too much to bear," borne
nonetheless, invisible weight too weak to nudge
a rowan-leaf but has broken backs, hearts, minds.
What I hear is music for Vadim Borisovskii,
viola-player. Borisovskii's dead. The viola sings.

TO AN ENGLSH COMPOSER

Landscapes flourish best
indoors. Here's one
you turned into music, green
in lush dissonance with green,
forty years ago. It glows

again. I carry it among
unEnglish rocks and rain
thinking - real English fields
would also lie untouched
by this ghost they fed. It flows

through fields and memories
of fields that gave and then forgot
and now rest weightless,
real ghosts that fail to touch
this burgeoning pastoral
with their mundane repose.

THE STORY OF KASPAR HAUSER

What he felt, dreamt, saw, thought he saw:
wind in ripe grain, wind through a copse
howling in a tunnel without walls or roof.
Silent rage. Peace beyond understanding.
The empty brain he left his inquisitors
refused to echo. Neither peace nor rage nor peace.
Buds on a dead tree? Song in a warped flute?
Not by sawing the wood, not by cursing the breath.

GRASS

A wind, for one moment, as if
for one moment someone listened.
Years to come are still in place.
Infinity has not disturbed
the seeding heads of grass. Never
still - even without wind
they invent some and nod in it.

WINTER TRAINS

Luggage, empty coats at rest.
No great demands. This
we ask - quiet wheels, move
for us now and all day.

Someone wonders why the Last
Things always come first.
Someone wishes the train were going
the other way. Always someone.

The trees are especially still.
A glance from one of them can last
and last, melt the ice and reach,
like spring moisture, remotest leaves.

NOT LOST

Autumn gale. Creation ruffled
the wrong way.
Leaves still on trees turn
their backs in millions. Leaves on the loose
panic, ambushed by nothing.

Time for memory to clear.
Nothing's lost,
like last year's leaves. Look:
a moment's undarkness gives
a hymn-tune, a scent of moor,

highland grass stroked, a wild
rose nudged,
a breeze reaching me across
thirty years. We can say
to this lucid welcome, "Welcome."

JUST AFTER THE SHORTEST DAY

Not much to see of the world
we thought we knew. What if all
creation were this one road
and the snow in this frail
man-made glare we bring
with us, our hope, our twin-star?

Knowledge we once had would give:
height – high, direction – west.
These are now Articles
of Doubt. Now it must be
an Article of Faith that seeds
wait in outer darkness beside us

all coded to produce, in time,
Mountain Eyebright, white,
Snow Cinquefoil, yellow,
Sedge, russet, Sorrel, red,
and the harebell, gentle
blue cup of memories.

WAKEFUL, THIRTY YEARS AGO

On bad nights, the clock:
one plus one plus one,
heaven as bad as hell
and not one touch
of God's breath to puff
away the acrid must
of church wood, the spores
never to be stopped
by Presbyterian green
soap and pine-polish,
the spores that settle unto
death in wind-pipe
and irreplaceable lungs.
On bad nights I saw
lichen come alive
in my soul's moist cracks:
no human chance
against biology
with The Old Testament
at hand to pack its punch.

On good nights, the clock:
counting out the hours
torn by strath winds,
waiting for the next
shudder of solid walls
gave comfort. The space
I half slept in,
made secure by storms,
was an inner weather
clean as light is clean.
I would imagine God
as a candle-flame
fragile in extremis
but inextinguishable.

On good nights I saw
my hands young, middle-
aged and old at once.
The still-living wood
of the sycamore that creaked
nursed me back to sleep.

A JEWISH CEMETERY

It's over-filled, leaning stones
about to panic, a crowd in mid
flight, a desperate push
out. No room for the dead,
who now must occupy
as narrow space as spirits do.

And the weight. Europe slopes in
towards such gathering points,
over-crowdings of death. They hold
our continent in place.
Imagine: anchors solid as breath,
chains cumbersome as light.

TRAVELLING, TO AN OLD PLACE

The first night. A sea without waves.
A sky with too many stars. They throng
in, fresh anonymous millions.
The first day. No prevailing wind.
A nation of bare trees leaning east
by habit. By habit too this patient
February waiting. Hard buds
beyond counting swell in soft mist.

The second night. A sea refusing still
to move as seas do. Towards dawn
a hatchwork of inch-long strokes,
horizon to horizon, drawn by one
immeasurable silent breath.
The second day. Sudden white lakes
of snowdrops under winter's brushwood.

The third night. Headlamps at speed.
Out of the city, into the city. Each
pair saying "I am the universe."
So many. Such speed. I think
from planes we must look small and slow.
The third day. Footsteps, footsteps, like
a slow-motion downpour of rain.
They overcrowd narrow streets between
medieval walls. They eddy round
preserved small churches, cubes of kept
silence. I enter one. The silence is
older than the oldest forest. It adds
my few footfalls to its archive.

The fourth night. I dream obsessively
of old doors opening, one by one.

MULTITUDES

Crows, blackening a dead elm.
They wait. Sparrows, sudden shade
on cathedral walls. They pass.

At night, we remember day-
time crowds. We follow the turns
medieval lanes take us.

No-one else out. It's the dead
who see us home, tomorrow
they will throng round us again.

Our footprints and theirs match. It's
by their absence the dead give
countless presence to our steps.

INFRA-RED PHOTOGRAPH

These Cambridge walls met
four centuries ago
and they're still tête-à-tête.
A many-branching creeper, loop
within loop, is so massed
it's like the human family tree.

Film sees retreats the eye
can't. Coaxed out in darkness,
leaves, flowers, incandesce,
walls are pliant, petal-thin.
Time is translucent at last.
Eternity is seeping in.

MESSAGES IN SPRING

Dried sunflowers, stored
light. We don´t shake off
old seasons overnight.

Old music for a new day;
"iam hiems transiit,"
earth is blossoming again.

Telephone wires are humming:
a haze of clarity, a dis-
harmonious unison.

News of death, a black seed
has won against the odds and found
a new season´s fertile ground.

MORNING WORDS

"In memoriam" - that too
is brought to light by this red
sun hugely clearing tree-tops.

Nothing stays clear. Snowflakes bring,
"ad infinitum," heaven
to earth. Many become one.

I, one, escape from many
dream-egos: "timor vitae"
makes them hesitate and hide.

I set hidden music free.
A loud voice from 1610
reaches out. "Exultavit."

TIME-KEEPERS

Nine chimneys, nine
shadowy clock-hands
turning on the red tiles,
shortening towards noon,
lengthening towards dusk,
their arc narrowing into winter,
widening into summer again -
unfailing, as time goes.
As time goes, they stop short

always. Even on sunny days
they leave a wedge untouched,
a missing keystone, a blank,
a secret they refuse to cross.
Of overcast days, of nights
when stars pace out depths
above roofs, and beneath roofs
dreams throng like city crowds,
they have no recollection.

REACHING LÜBECK

Cobblestones, a mile
of smooth handiwork
a century old
now leading nowhere.

Towers welcome us.
They say: "Heaven is
still high. Some of us
are still pointing up."

EASTER SUNDAY WINDOWS

One of them we sit by now.
Outside: mist so dense the world
is as good as gone. Only
this edge of a wooden barn
with a grandfatherly date
is left. Is this nature being
at odds again with things we
want to celebrate? The mist
absorbs the light, gives none back.

Inside: daffodils and lit
yellow candles. They give a
newly-risen whiteness to
our skins. Later, when the sun
has ransacked the wide landscape's
closest inch, we will recall
these gentle flames. We will find
them burning still, giving light
where nature says there is none.

LASTING

One kind of immortality.
Pale boulders, indigestible
in this thin landscape, are piled
like gross frames round each square
of soil. These are the memorials
of the many lives worn out harvesting stones.

Another kind. Prodigality,
again nature's. Thousands of white
anemones, thousands of green
almost-open birch-leaves, a white
haze of grave gentleness, a green
haze of joy, those minutes that outlast stones.

REQUIEM

Someone else's sorrow made
music. Voices many years
dead are singing in my room,
bringing back the grief that held
someone else for life. They pass
cloud-like over landscapes long
worn: their shadows brighten, not
darken, everything they touch.

DURING A FINAL ILLNESS

Enclosing summer mist - no
far-sightedness today:
saplings tower, leaves have hands
larger than life. New grass
says: "We have earth enough."
A gorse-bush in full blaze:
"I have leisure in which to burn."
It burns without being consumed.
Its yellow flame owes nothing
to this mist and my passing
soul, both of which it lights up.

WHAT THE COLOURS SAID
A Song

BLUE said the blue sky
I am fathomless,
I will burn your brain
through, you will drown in
deeper deeper blue.

YELLOW said the wide
dandelion field,
I will burn your brain
too, despite closed eyes
yellow will blind you.

LISTEN said the high
tight telephone wire,
I will make your brain
sing with me until
your nerves are like mine.

PALE said the night sky,
I am the fathoms
beyond fathomless
blue. GREY said the shut
dandelion field.

LISTEN said the wire
still awake, our nerves
are in unison,
BLACK will not muffle
such singing as ours.

LANGUAGES

Latin, for the mind's
own good; for stained glass
shining the day long.
NEC TAMEN was stamped
on all my Sundays.

Gaelic, for hill-tops.
It is remembered
as the autumn strath
is, in winter, its
heathery soft flame.

English, for sermons,
shops, the waiting world.
Forebears carried it
like an emigrant's
old-fashioned suitcase.

TWO PICTURES ON MY WALL

First, a photograph: iron-railing tops,
pointed, formidable;
one angular starved tree, or tree-outline,
as much life as iron;
in the distance, across water, shadows
in the grain - Manhattan.

Then, a water-colour: hill, heather, loch,
all a shade too coloured
for the quiet shades that quicken live moors;
it's Loch Araichlin, so
remote from roads it could lip-lap lip-lap
through four seasons unseen.

Side by side. They look like open secrets.
I think of two scale-pans,
on one side nothing, on one too much, yet
the trembling needle says
"equal." It's their silence makes me listen,
what they hide makes me look.

VISITING YOUR DEATH

*

Sailing westwards towards your death
I watch mist annul the North Sea
horizon. That ochre gleam is
the sun you will not see again.
Your death is shining in the sea.

*

Looking down from a high window
on the first Sunday of your death
I see how the sycamore leaves
let waste not one ray of sunlight.
"Sanctus." Slender chimes overlap.

*

Driving northwards into brightness
that is your death, I find only
sharp hill-lines, high razor-edge trees,
blue air like more-than-human sight.
My sadness turns white like a cloud.

*

At last, by your newly closed grave,
have I lost you on my way here?
You are now at your most distant.
We are at the summer solstice,
your presence, your absence, equal.

*

"Nec tamen consumebatur"
shone as long as the daylight did
behind your high polished pulpit.
Your mortality first touched you
where you were strong. It touched your words.

*

The night wind tossing the cornflowers
disturbs my memories of you.
Are the flowers still blue in the dark?
Are you still deaf to the rustle
of leaves? Will morning not find you?

*

I visited your death. Your death
visited me with the kind clear
light of a coppery moonrise.
It shines over the happiness
and the sadness waiting for me.

HOMAGE TO A GARDENER

Why call them "weeds"? Look:
dandelion fields, willow-herb hillsides,
lupin embankments
(primitive blue, predating the hybrids).
Even in gardens
nothing is quite tamed. Take chrysanthemums
("gold-flowers" to Greeks)
disintegrating nostalgically
in autumn suburbs,
shreds of mellow colours on misty days,
outlasting shrunk leaves,
surviving also the first rimy dawns.

Father might have said
"A bonny sight," not bothering to add
"but..." He would have thought
nature is too prolific, impatient;
refine, select, prune,
wait, outwit frosts, earwigs, north winds, south winds.
Each plant gave its all,
concentrated itself, to one stem, one
ponderous blossom.
Cut, they shone from October to Christmas,
preserved autumn suns.
Thus far nature gave in to art. He let
neither win outright.
He saved from real gold's perennial death
the colour of gold,
a ripeness that would not refuse to die.
He saved from nature
something choice, more-than-nature, incarnate.

NOT YET

Cornflower thicket,
long past its season.
Pull it up? Not yet.
The last miniature
cobalt survivors
who arrived too late
hang on. I watch them
as if they were frail
unwritten gospels,
rare first-born from whom
much might have been hoped.

UNQUIET HIGHLAND LANDSCAPE

Grasses on the ruffled slopes of Loth
all summer spend
their seed and their voices in the wind.
On the raised beach
pale stones gather silence and keep it.

In a green slope under Bunnilidh
after your last
crossing of the many-voiced river
you gather now
not words but these our new silences.
You hoard nothing:
more generous than immortal stones
you give back our silences many-fold.

NOON STANDSTILL

This blue midday September sky
is immovable, holds the earth
in place. Some of the dead I know
were not finished admiring it.

CLOUD AND SEED

White solitary evening cloud
bulging like a city adrift.
Hard not to admire you. Yet not
one pin could dance on your soft crown.

From ground level I watch you float.
Between us, a silhouetted
row of stalks with withered-in, black-
dwarfish, hob-nobbing dense pin-tops.

Extremes meet. The vigorous dead
crowd round me just before my birth,
just after my death. I'm both young
and old. Both cloud-big and seed-small.

MARREL HILL

I would have said
of Marrel Hill
"a parental presence:"
abstracted moods,
surprises like weather,
and always there.

I would have said.
But now this year
"a parental presence"
is locked in soil
washed down from Marrel Hill
and its strath kin.

I could say, his
absence will now
outlast rocks. I could say
it's his presence
that robs the crumbling hill
of its longevity.

LAST VIEWS

The sea heard but not seen.
Much of the world blocked out
by a neighbour's slate roof.
Smoke from coal-fires lounging
at all hours. Marrel Hill
an eternal presence
not much noticed - but if
one morning it had gone,
what absence! The small view
lit by a new skyline
would be a second life
invading one we knew.
It would shine like the white
unreadable old face
of a clock without hands.

WOOD FIRE AND SUMMER RAIN

Dried birch - it should
have waited till winter.
Here it is now
cracking, spitting out scent.
The black stove creaks,
soon unseasonally
too hot to touch.
Bowed, soaked, disconcerted
sunflower heads
hang outside the window
in day-long rain.
They could be last year's dead
looking in on
scenes that no longer fit
- so suddenly -
their composed memories.

IN MY DREAM

Glassy leaves on the birch at the far edge
of the third field chipped against each other.
The three musicians sat on high-backed chairs
by the first field. They played to the bare field.
There was enough autumn light left for them
to play to the second field then the third.
The melodies they played healed the cut fields
of all the hurt fruitfulness had brought them.

MÅRUP CHURCH
(North West Denmark)

It is not a ruined poorhouse out at the edge of
 life, but a church, and it was once at the centre.
 Human tides have ebbed inland and the sea is
 eating at the earthy cliff. Juniper bushes, with
 their long lives, and sea-pinks, with their short
 lives, never stop trembling.
In the churchyard old family graves are fenced in
 like box-pews. Gravestones are boulders taken
 up from the shore and inscribed: merchants
 who survived, captains and boys who went down.
The living come out here often and read the names
 of the dead. Some of the living are old and need
 help. They stoop and point. Inside the church,
 which smells like an abandoned barn, someone
 has left a pair of spectacles on the bare altar.

CAN'T STOP

I've been rushing away from your death
ever since then.
I wanted to stop still by your death
with the patience
trees spend on one part of a landscape.
I still do. I
am not without that kind of patience.
Caught in a dream
endlessly undreamlike, the landscape
hurries past, must
follow the timetable to your death.
Wrong way! Too late! I'm on the wrong train
rushing away from, not to, your death.

AUGUST 1920

Surprised? Of course, finding clouds
so unhistorical, white
and quick; and hedgerows chock full
and loud; and murmuring corn
about to yellow; cool pale
about-to-ripen Pippins,
Sweet Cox's, Golden, Ribston;

and children knowing not much
and adults knowing too much
ambushed by summer's fulness
and wishing it would stop short
and hold its blue, its bright green;
and not a trace of brown tint
that makes our photographs sad:

and Over There, where so much
had stopped short, somehow still far
away, "abroad," and far back
enough for those with sad cause
to count and say "It's two years
or three since then," the war gone
to ground beneath a tight nerve;

and further north than these dales
in Edinburgh, May Scott
(who married William Fulton)
not yet a widow; her son
my father John a month less
than twelve; in Thurso, not ten
quite, Margaret Macpherson;

the certainty of my flesh
improbable as dog-rose,

convolulus or speedwell
deciding: "That's enough. Let's
stop short and keep our sap moist.
The grandson, old, shall smell what
his father's father smelt, young."

TRAVELLING SOUTH, LOOKING NORTH

Beinn a´Bhragie´s wide south slope,
bright blaze of gorse, a curtain -
behind you I leave
a not very old gravestone,
and a white widow, waving.

TIDE

The tide is deathless in
the harbour where I drown
in dreams. It always ebbs
and sets small boats at rest
on silt, but always flows
and brings small boats to life
again;
it swells the river back
upon itself, it makes
the shallows deep, it sends
a slow darkness upstream
a mile at least and past
that walled and special field.
You lie
among parishioners
of thirty years. A few
you christened, some you wed,
and many you have seen
to earth: the words you said
for those
have now been said for you.

LANDSCAPE WITH VERTICALS

First, and tallest, the radio-mast, with giant suckers or owl-eyes, sifting the current. It has strong nerves, and room for multitudes. It can do nothing with silence.

Second, the tapering spire. It says "Not many, but one." It distills words into a concentrate: "Laus Deo" from one angle, "Ora pro nobis" from another.

Third, the maple, whose left side doesn't know what its right side is doing. Each autumn the left side is yellow when the right is still green, and when the left is leafless, the right is still yellow.

Fourth, and lowest, the bronze crucifix. Each hand knows what the other has suffered.

A FALSE DREAM

The church is squat beneath high sycamores.
Ivy has no chance. Why does he point then
across the strath: "You′ll remember the church?"
"That was never there!" He smiles as if I′ve
been away too long. Edges of crumbling
ochre like walls I saw in Avignon,
mostly a cliff of ivy. "That′s like me!
Nothing left to mourn." The words are too large.
He hated largeness.
What do I say to father who is not
father? "You′re a short-circuit in my brain.
The right face, the right voice, but the wrong style."
In true dreams the dead
are always in character. This false dream
I pray will not persist like a record
coming round with the, coming round with the

THE GREEN BOAT, THE NIGHT WIND
AND THE BIRCH

An inner harbour. Black, still, deep.
A long way
round I have to go, the more
time I take the more I need
to reach you - why are you aboard
an old green
fishing-boat, as if we had
urgent reasons to be gone?
You haven't noticed how the boat
has edged out
leaving silent fatal inches
I can't jump or swim, between.

A world I am about to lose
when dry night
wind cascades like rivers on
moonlit roofs. It says "You're here."

The birch behind the house has lost
its last leaf.
Something else I could have watched.
Something else the dead won't see.

UNCOLLECTED 1976-1990

A WORD FOR A WORD

Perhaps the wind was first, howling THIS
when the kitchen door slammed shut with THAT.
"How I wonder what you are!" I did,
so much stared back that seemed to know.
Or roads in summer with their slow WHERE
or mountain streams, impatient WHEN
or pale snow with its IS and EVER SHALL.

I grew. IF, ALTHOUGH, BECAUSE, EXCEPT
left little room for certainty
still less EITHER-OR. I came
to grief at double negatives despite
proverbs nodding like vague aunts:
"A word in time saves nine," or "Don't
use one word where none will do."

I sat still and became a common noun
in danger of suffocation by adjective.
I walked free, an active present verb
soon to lose my sense of person and time
faced with such tempting conjugations.
I acted dumb, stooped in a question-mark,
posed in quotes, hid between brackets.

I shook hands with strangers - would anything
feel the same again? And I learned to hear
behind my own "birch": "björk, "Birke,"
"bouleau, "beryoza," "bhurja," "betula"
and "koivu" like a cold visitor.
Are the ghosts more real, am I to see
whiter white greener green than mine?

"The sound of silence," I think, secure
dreaming back to THIS and THAT and IS,
trees that are "only" trees, peace in a crowd -

but not where the ghosts are real, demand
affection, pardon, facts, facts. They stare
as if my mother-tongue were old tattoos.
I laugh. It's not funny, in a foreign tongue

to break a silence I say: "There was a fly
lived in my car, a fellow-traveller all
the way from Baden Baden to Stockholm,
said nothing, nothing to declare."
Neither had I. Speechless across worn
rebuilt Europe. Traffic-lights,
indicators, road numbers in order.

There are limits then: we learn to give
silent welcome. My present tense grows
longer and longer shadows. Some sound
that will refuse speech follows me.
I know it will refuse. It always has.
Perhaps the wind was first, a perfect fifth
above the darkened river's silent ground.

(1976)

THINGS COMING BACK

Old snow is stubborn, shrinks, hardens, shrinks,
reveals, not all at once but I did see,
where drifts had been, keels of wintered boats.

I think of this one morning when rank
labyrinths of dream close under me.
I waken to acute loss of memory.

I think of this too passing a graveyard
with wide green spaces waiting. I imagine
trying to read a page no-one has written on.

What started this was our sitting here
as if we'd been nowhere. And one of us said
"Remember Mount Lemon, how we never got?"

(1978)

ARRAN HAIKU

Crushed grass in the thirties. An
extinct bird, Avro Anson,
drills soft clouds over Arran.

Bharrain, Bhreac, Tarsuinn,
Nuis, Goat Fell. They made
huge clouds trickle down quiet glens.

Whiting Bay. Full cups
of rhododendron
waited to be touched and spilt.

Corrie. A name heard
like a bell from lips
of wet home-coming adults.

Blackwaterfoot. Grey
hulking warships, short-
lived cathedrals in the mist.

Shiskine. Black and white keys trained
at Mozart. Wet colours ran
down tall streaming manse windows.

(c. 1980)

AFTER ASH WEDNESDAY

Someone has opened a window
    that was shut for seven months.
Fields are being scrutinised, inch by
    inch they widen into steppes.
Minutes are longer than hours. In
    garden corners brushwood has
no secrets to keep. The leafless
    trees are side-lit, shine like white
glass, and people who walk among
    them look like pale invalids.
Everyone ambushed by brightness,
    spring, exposure, chill surprise.
Spaces are waiting. The padlocked
    church is packed with light at dawn.

(1984)

GOOD FRIDAY IN EINBECK

In Einbeck the bell
drops each heavy hour
in our rippling pool of sleep.

From three, before light
a blackbird winds and
winds himself in his echo.

From five, rain, the hush
of waves in a shell.
For eight hundred years the earth

has been hidden by
town-square slabs and fronts.
At seven, organ music

prowls, a sad tiger,
Good Friday's song rest-
less behind blind streaming stone.

(1989)

THE DEAD IN DREAMS

They come and go, like anyone else.

Father came regularly for two and a half years after his death. He said very little to me for he was usually busy. Still, I was glad to see him. Then one night he spoke to me directly and seriously, and referred for the first time to his condition. But I was perplexed, for while the face and voice were his, the melodramatic gestures were quite out of character and I doubted if the dream could be a true one. He talked about something being "quite finished" and told me there was nothing to mourn. After that he stayed away for at least three months.

When he did return he was in a hurry. He sealed two envelopes at his desk in the old manse and without turning round left the room and went to the kitchen from where his voice could be heard telling mother about someone he had met in the village. If he had turned round he would have seen me.

(1987)

HE HAS COME BACK

The manse and garden seem to be surrounded by a high brown wall. Because the night is so dark I can see only parts of the wall, in the light of paraffin lamps held to windows. The wall follows a complicated pattern with many corners, dividing the garden into deep chasms. It has given the wind a new note, a more hollow accent to its familiar voice in the bare sycamores and apple-trees and the solitary pine. How can I have lived here for so long without seeing the wall?

Despite the wind, I hear a car on the pebbles of the driveway, the scrape and bang of garage doors. Surprising how smoothly the 1934 Woolsley is still running in 1985. In he comes. He has his 1950s face - firm, nothing shrunk - and straight shoulders. His black minister's tweed coat brings indoors whiffs of salt air, petrol, tobacco. Before eating, he says, he wants to inspect the leeks to make sure that the wind hasn't damaged them. He goes out into one of the chasms, carrying a black chunky wartime bicycle-lamp with an angular hood.

He has come back. The howling of the wind makes the inside of the house feel secure.

(1985)

THE THREE OF US

Age does not divide us, or so people say when they are not old. But it's true, sometimes.

Grandmother (mother's mother) lived at 59 Princes Street, Thurso, a house of Caithness stone whose greyish brown colour is so much part of the landscape it is hard to believe the house didn't grow there naturally.

Here we are, the three of us, sitting at a card-table on the pavement outside the house. Grandmother died about twenty years ago, and father eighteen months ago. As usual, cherry-cake has appeared from a magic tin.

The garden at the back of the house, unseen by passers-by, is nothing to speak of and the cultivation of flowers is not one of her gifts, but she tells us something we have never heard before: the flowers in her little plot have supernaturally intense colours, blue more blue than blue, yellow more yellow than yellow. Every summer the miracle repeats itself and neighbours ask for cuttings to see if the same results can be achieved in their own gardens. But the miracle doesn't work in other gardens. Father, who knows more than most about the cultivation of flowers, is astonished. He laughs at himself for not having noticed.

(1985)

II

FOR SOMETHING LIKE A SECOND

It's weeks now, I thought,
since they've noticed me.
The dead, I meant. That night, then -
I'm fifty but back
where once I was five.
From the manse window I watch
a flat-topped beech-hedge
(which was never there)
and beyond it the black pools
(which were) flooded up
from The Black Water.
Father, gone four years, is back
too, but not thirty,
more like seventy,
ruffled, tired in the morning.
We're out of time with
time and place. Our years
slide, bits of broken mirror.
But for something time
would call a second
we're in time with each other.
Beyond the crisp hedge
the unmoved black pools
turn white, answering the sky.

CHILDHOOD

"God who made the earth"
father sang.
Indoors, Germany calling.
Outside, peace and rain.

GARDEN

Take this empty dream
garden, sycamore
grey. Abruptly then
father. "You're dead!" "Touch!"
All next day I felt
the tweed of his sleeve.

HELMSDALE

Cow-parsley. Pushy
rough-featured, at large
between unattended walls.
That day its sweetness
got the better of
harbour salt, village-street coal.

FAMILY

A bible, a block
of choking spice from
1856. Its end-
papers are crumbling
into the crowded
silent lines of births and deaths.

ONE OF OUR PRESENT TENSES

If we had been there so long ago
upstairs on an orange-and-green tram
past the locked park, its wild irises.
The moist slopes we thought we could still find
forty years later.
Those who are old when we are now young
wait in bread queues. Their houses are rubbed
shabby, worn down by war bulletins.
We give our farthings to the unshaved
mouth-organ player.
Peace has brought more lamps on nights of fog.
We are too fresh yet to be rubbed down.
If we had been there. Those tram windows
are stubbornly open, we lurch through
waves of hawthorn scent.

THE BELL
Kloster Andechs

The centre of this universe pealed noon.
On the sundial death and an angel held
up UNA EX HISCE MORIERIS.

Off-centre, a beer garden. The hot crowds
balanced the unequal weights of their lives.
Their nervous hands asked where they could add more.

Across the fields ripe grain hissed: "We're one seed.
Count us." All afternoon the bell gave out
its five loaves and two fishes, its silence.

ICON

Music comes from the darkness, the left hand.
The right hand, holding the violin bow,
is so pale it's about to incandesce,
like the pale bird with open wings striding
on the right shoulder. On the mauve left knee
(crossed on the right) two birds, one green, one blue,
rest, facing left, right. Flowers hang from heaven.
We see all of the right cheek - it's fiery.
We see little of the left - it's chilled, grey.
The right eye's too big and it sees too much.
It's blue. The left eye's a red scar. It's blind.
The violin's body glows like ripe grain.
Around the roofs sleeping beneath his feet
the blue night air is beaded with music
from the left fingers, the touchers of strings,
the perfume-givers. The left hand's not there.

THE WATERMARK

The white light of the afternoon waves
throngs in.
The voices crowd in too, leaving no
corner
of air unagitated in this
creaking
wooden room whose windows ancestors
measured
to fit their view of unmeasured ocean.

Oblongs of piled rocks on the shore mark
common
graves. The ornaments survived the skulls.
From these
stones a light shines further than our eyes
can hold.
It is hard and survives ornaments.
It glows
through me to the unread watermark
I bear
from window to window and never see.

I TAKE MY WAY BACK

I take my way through sweet-smelling pines.
I am whole, I count my many years,
they add up to one. Each warm pine says:
"I am one as well, I have my rings."
A rush-hour sparrow-pack crowds a branch,
their argument sounds like panic, like
"all-or-nothing, all-or-nothing, all - "

A death I know of like an eclipse
briefly passed over part of the sky
beyond my sight. A green field I saw
this morning is now being loaded with
one more absence. The sunlight is sharp:
the shadows worn by those still alive
must be so thin they'd tear like tissue.

I am no longer whole, though my years
still fit me like resinous rings. Half
blinded I take my way back, count and
lose count, then let warm trees walk with me,
blind leaders. Their cargo of birdsong
spills on me. The half of my shadow
I can see is dusted with pollen.

PERFECTIONISTS

Sparrows chip at their statue-in-progress,
the air. Shoals of leaf-shadows nudge and nudge.
Those baking stones will never becomes loaves.
Pines sweat resin, would like to walk but can´t.

The dead, those doers of nothing -
they are perfectionists, I always have one or
another of them by me. The cool vast
calm they spread, like waters I can run on.

LOOKING WEST FROM HÅ

A white wall. Two paintings facing in, slabs
of Italian mauve. Between, a window,
a live picture, narrow never still life
of boulder landscape with over-sized sky.
Behind wall and window, in a white light,
The North Sea shouldering its way nowhere.
Behind nowhere, Duncansby Head. Behind
that, turning small corners between green slopes,
Thurso River, as if there were no sea.

MY RIVERS

The Black Water, how
thin a rivulet
to have taught me four
seasons. It follows
me still round each year.
On my private map
its course is bold, un-
deterred by creases.

The Cart would watch me
balance my nine years
on its slimy clay.
Beneath lonely oaks
I hid in its noise
from lonely suburbs -
adults and windows.
Hours that failed to grow.

The Tweed was father`s.
It was a frontier.
Behind his boyhood
roamed Victorian,
Edwardian aunts,
uncles. Life-stories
swarmed out of hearing.
I was unheard-of.

Thurso River we
shared, father and I.
Hours that have now grown
spacious like full years.
How light its voice was,
how unencumbered
by generations
of hare-bell and cloud.

Helmsdale River, he
listened to that voice
for thirty-six years
and its soft debate
now runs past his grave.
It will never be
resolved. That river
has poured loneliness

through me. I visit
its source now and then.
Something shies away.
I pretend then I'm
concentrating on
the wind's low whispers
in hazels, the high
complaints of curlews.

AUTUMN STORM

Night. The tree semaphores black on black.
My window can't choose, takes what it must.
Its page of score is full. I hear that
not-quite-music spill from stave to stave.

I remember one of my rivers:
its shaky line holds for centuries.
In its narrow course the river shows
its fill of unmeasured Caithness sky.

I lack the straight sides of the window
and the river's eloquent surface.
The globe sends gate-crashers: I'm helpless.
The globe turns its smooth back: I'm empty.

Morning. The tree leans with, I against
the gale. My slow partner and I use
roots differently. Bole and spine test how
to bargain with brash new contingents.

THOSE WHO'LL STAY

Sparrows. Brown snow-flakes in a hurry.
Sudden fruit bending a bare bush. Gone.

Gulls, high, falling up, climbing down, slow-
motion debris from a distant blast.

Geese who aimed themselves south are now runes.
They breathe the sky of wonder emblems.

Winter, runeless, opens a large eye
on those who'll stay. His handclasp is tight.

SHOSTAKOVITCH OPUS 122

The voices of the four strings are forest voices.
Thin seconds snap.
Boles are nourished on the moist patience of decades.
In my dream I have to grow old beyond my span

and then I can hear the silence that follows me
through the loud wood.
The silence says: "I'm the third party, the witness,
this music you hear runs over my careful hands."

In my dream that is not a dream the music says:
"I didn't knock
but you opened to me." It sings infallibly
in my failing distracted backbone. The trees wait.

SHOSTAKOVITCH OPUS 144

I think it was a shore where all the rocks
were smooth. They had outlived so much the wind
could find no edge to heighten its complaint.

I think he must have been here. I eavesdrop
on music not written for listeners.
The four strings share out their small silences.

Dissonance he brought with him. And the blocked
views down paths where friends had vanished. A world
of sharp edges had almost unmade him.

Here he remade it, then went back to it.
I warm my hands on cold stone. He was here.
It was a shore where all the rocks were smooth.

BRITTEN'S *LACHRYMAE*

A late afternoon January sun
hazy as cottonwool, incandescent
through the unsolved riddles of birch thickets.

Decades ago the young master (dead now)
made his reflections on the old master
(centuries dead). We look in his mirror.

Scarce visible theme haunts variations:
spectral forefather. A last-minute face
of mercy blinding from dissonances.

ONE-PART INVENTION
(On a theme of Peter Huchel)

This crowded page of score:
notes, a population
stopped in mid-step at noon,
photographed from high up.

Or: the ancient rough braille
of a hill stream's bedrock.
The music obeys, flows
freed by obedience.

Then this honeysuckle
tendril: its shadow writes
one mandarin sign on
each page. Its alphabet

has one sharp character,
its language one locked word.
It would leave breath, fingers,
waiting above reeds, keys.

TWO-PART INVENTION
(*On a theme of Sarah Kirsch*)

We are whole only
in the bird's head, you
in its southern, me
in its northern eye.

I was blind, I watched
September: warm breath
of willow-herb, sharp
blue eye on still tarns.

I was deaf, the birch
woke me. Already
its night-long voices
were in dark archives.

I lost my balance.
My right hemisphere
shed its last red leaf
and now had no weight.

In the brain of one
migrating swift I
was seen to be whole:
my right hand had found

shadows, leaves and words,
my left hand had moved
like a torch through that
blind left hemisphere.

THREE-PART INVENTION
(On a theme of Grete Tartler)

As if a leaf shifted
from left to right, from one
paving stone to the next.
As if a shiver passed
from your flesh to the flesh
of your alter ego.
As if two great mirrors
rushed at you, first to blind
then to crush you between.

I like to find a third.
Some unlined lake-surface
that would bear crowding feet.
Some three's-company, close
presence of the dead, that
thin untearable screen,
silky, warm on both sides.
Some prism to fan out
the splendours of darkness.

As if I could touch them -
Vergil to Statius:
"Shade you are, shade you see."
Statius: "I forget,
through love, our emptiness,
treating shade as solid."
This observed by a third,
whose limbs broke the sun's rays,
whose weight made pebbles slide.

THE INHERITANCE

It was time to share out the three houses.
The first, of white stone, had its private trees.
The second, of stained brick, was crowded in.
The third, a shack on a crumbling cliff-edge.

Since I was the first-born I had first choice.
No-one said I was closest to death but
I took the worst and moved in, fearful of
an old-age chronically off-balance.

So near an edge I discovered an art
of steadiness. Think of a pair of scales,
one pan empty, the other piled with weights,
and the arm stays level. I was the arm.

My inheritance defied gravity.

RELEARNING RUSSIAN

It was his "waxy sputter" of blossom
from an old tree that would keep Pasternak
blindly present, present continuous.

Bruised by grammar the stranger is dazzled
straining to see that sticky window-pane
from inside. Past tenses are sliding traps:

pluperfect may be waiting for you through
innocent glass. Like this dream - the icon
whose blind Virgin's name was Perestroika.

The silver was kissed thin by good and bad.
The grey icon was not silver but steel.
It was not an icon but a helmet.

HIGHLAND PEBBLE

In the hand, found wanting.

There are more ways to growth
than obeying green cells.

In dreams I throw the stone
and it walks back. In life
I throw it and it stops.

In neither can I lift
what gives the stone its weight:
Ben Griam's westward scoop,
the wind's prevailing touch

and the tenacity
of water molecules
working through the peat maze.

A context, outliving.
A subtext, blind, writ large.

My hand, that's found wanting.

WINDOWS

"Windows - without them
the rain's eloquence
would be wasted on deaf walls."

I wrote those twelve words
in innocence and
trouble-free weather. Tonight

father, now years dead,
raps my black window.
He has found his lost fury.

HEIGHTS

Above the roof, how many skies. The first so
shallow gulls avoid it; they stamp a wet field.
The second so
deep our eyes invent a surface and rest there.

The third has a population of oak leaves
no two identical. The fourth holds its breath
while a curlew
imitates madness. The fifth assumes deafness

and sends back everything we ask it. The sixth
invites our highest numbers to dance neatly
on a pin-head.
The seventh bends oceans with its heavy hand.

The roof behaves like Alpha and Omega.
Its definiion of us does not include
windows or doors.
Out of habit a deft wind tests each corner.

VAUGHAN WILLIAMS – ONE OF HIS TUNES

A hood of sunlight
has been pulled over my head.

The last of the world
I saw was a white wall stained
green, dead wood's second
death. Rain shut its heavy door.

In the hood I climb
like a line of song down warm
cliffs. They are neither
mineral nor animal.

Gravity stops me
falling. I know gravity
will help me to rise.
I move with the assurance

of a rope-walker
who has taught his rope to think,
for whom neither right
nor left has further terror.

The music is tough.
The song's inventor is dead:
long before he died
he sang in his hood of light.

STRATH

On the pavements of Schwabing or Karlsfelt

my insteps remember the give of peat
climbing from Suisgill Burn near Kilphedir
where the rain-drifts divide.

I have faithful shadows, they are lighter
not darker, they shine wherever they touch
implementing daylight.

The strath has no use for inhabitants,
its chief occupation is the transport
of whispering water.

If it had language its variations
on green and brown would fill dictionaries.
Its plant life is thigh-deep

in bracken, ankle-deep in heather, skin-
deep in lichen. Its news concerns the size
and speed of cloud-shadows.

The strath renews itself in me like cells.
If I walk there my insteps brace, long for
the foreign crowdedness

of Schwabing or Karlsfelt.

THE VILLAGE

I wore it lightly. Not by choice:
a role, I said, I can unlearn,
a shadow I can fold away.

When I stopped hearing the quarters
from the war-memorial clock
my left arm became hard to raise.
When the manse was cleared out, then filled
by an alien's furniture,
my right arm became hard to raise.
When I forgot the river's voice
at low tide beneath the stone bridge
my rib-cage needed all its strength.

All I had left was the harbour.
Its black high tide swelled up in dreams.
My feet were past hope of lifting.

NATIVE LAND

My place on earth, a crease in a worn map.
Ice-age boulders fill me from skin to skin.

So many counties to keep an eye on.
Decades are too busy to wait for me.

But how morning keeps coming back at it.
Side-lit, cliffs add weightlessness to their weight.

The cargo of houses, gravestones, lightens.
Pines relax their hold, don't lose their balance.

VERDUN

A stubborn haze seventy-four years thick.
I and old photos
stare at each other. I always blink first.

The town rides today's pasture and cornfields.
Indefensible.
It survives, as ships do, on the surface.

X's ranked acre by acre, order
not wished for in life.
Our crossed grandfathers have been straightened out.

HOME THOUGHTS

"Heimat" is for the long-sighted.
Behind the sea's curve, "hame" and "home."
"Hame" was a stranger's. "Home" was mine.
Roots I can't see are dividing
still. I imagine leafy mists.

I've come to someone else's "hjem."
The wind's voice in the summer birch
has found a thousand different ways
of saying "Listen." I listen.

Below it, the measured earth says
"I'm local, closed." It's wide open.
Above it, universal sky
says "Welcome, I'm unlimited."
The heavy blue shutters are locked.

I see garden walls round the birch,
a well of warmth for the wind's voice
to ripen in. I see nothing.
The voice takes its ripeness with it.

EQUINOX

They too
have birthdays, like this: dark
and light are for one day equal.

For us,
the living, September
sun is that magnesium flash
letting us still see our parents
inside their prewar photographs.

Greater
light is slammed by greater
darkness.

It seems.
That Tuscan, outside earth's
shadow, wondered and was answered,
"how, when made visible again,
such brightness will not pain one's sight."

He learned
how darkness has weak hands,
how the pain of light trains us for joy.

FROM A HISTORY OF MUSIC

"So many events have reached
their raison d´être along each stalk - "

"How tough each thread: airy
tons of biography are bouncing - "

"Defies the climate. Green leaves
invent sun when the other has hid - "

"Joy in the flotsam of cells.
Grace in the lumber of heavy roots - "

"Can´t they once stop and listen
to silence growing? Is this a dream?"

Someone has carved JSB
on bark now implacable as rock.

THURSO, JULY 1947

"Not this war but the one before."
Adults said so much. I choked too
on silence. Raw spelling-mistakes.

Friends of my grandfather's had lain
down in green fields. I dreamt that some
of their wounds were invisible.

Wind in the grass, the noise of life
near its beginning. A music
too slow and stubborn for humans.

It's not Life but lives that pace us.
We keep up with them or lose them.
Not yet being born, I saw nothing.

But three decades later I heard
the herring-man shout, and the clink-
scuff of horse-hooves on Princes Steet.

I heard the sounds that had waited.

SMALL WORLD

Those patches on the moon
that bothered Dante - here
above my right shoulder.
Sun, Septemberish, not
noticeably older
than it was in May; not
noticeably closer
to any edge of truth
because it meets me at
eye-level and hurts more.

This sycamore I´ve watched
for fifteen years would say
I scarcely count: would say
my sense of perspective
has unexplained shadows.
Above my left shoulder
Gordian knots of cloud
have been slashed: their flung shreds
are now permanent as
chafe-marks on ice-age rock.

FIVE-FINGER NOCTURNE

I thought we were old friends
my daytime wood and me.
We were. Seventeen years´
familiarity

though is displaced tonight
the first time I walk through
in darkness. Face-level
hand-breadths of silver bark

show the blackened surprise
of smiling skull faces
in negatives. Sharp stars
at pine-top height shine like

tiny Americas
discoverable for
the asking. A streetlamp
I never knew was there

shows at the wood edge: high
willow-herb stalks scribbled
all up and down in a
coiling feathery hand

furry white ink on black
paper. The seeds have gone.

INSIDE HISTORY

Where from, remote. Where to, remote. That
almost remote razory vapour-
trail cuts a white slit in blue skin. No
blood shows.

News like migrating fieldfares homes in
on a speck on the world's map, a house
whose furniture refuses to age.
Timbers

rest in their resinous perspectives.
Brass wheels in the clock have not noticed
the interruptions of history.
Or births.

Windows that have served generations
never discriminate between light
travelling in from the sun and light
from lamps

setting out. And when both sides are black
they allow darkness to flow freely
keeping its balance. They can still serve
thus those

next generations who have not yet
queued up.

SETTING OUT

The gravestones still weight the same.
No-one has altered the dates.

No-one asks why I've come back
again. To see not graves but

that wedge in the river-bank
where the green boat leaned. My years

at home had boulders on them.
The keel never touched water.

My years away tugged at weight
no longer there. The ribs then

gave their atoms slowly back.
The boat is no longer boat.

Its ghost sets out at high tide.
Its wake is a coiling script

whose fluency the words trapped
on granite could well envy.

ON THE OTHER SIDE OF LANGUAGE

Inside the rock-faced pine-bark
silent water-of-life climbs
cell by cell. It's not Babel.
No words: nothing to confuse.
The bark can't speak of water.
The high needles can't question
their singing-master the wind.

A man trapped outside language
struggles to break down his own
defences. To let words in.
He's alone. Soundless Babel.
A confusion of silence
that divides, chokes, divides, chokes.
Tree-rings that shrink and tighten.

A black spark no-one could see
started his private ice-age.
A dwindling tongue of ice dumps
boulders, his new alphabet.
Trees walk in the rain. He hears
music from their hopeful cells.
His mouth is bark, is tone-deaf.

INSIDE THE SPACIOUS TOMB

The white glow from the wakened corpse
brightens the faces of the two
staring angels, one left one right,
and the back of the third, who lifts
lightly the jagged square stone slab
from the tomb's round-arched opening.

The square never fitted the arch.
The reclining head is too small
and the legs too long. The whiteness
sees with the eyes of lightning things
that don't fit. It is eager. Soon
it will ambush the blind dawn trees

but already it has cut short
eighteen centuries and startled
Mr Blake in South Molton Street.

GOOD FRIDAY IN THE FIELDS OF DENMARK

On this day of the One Tree
I'm obsessed by the Many:
their elegant intricate
nakednesses crowd skylines.

Rooks' nests can hide nothing from
inspectorial sunlight.
Above fields which are now packed
with seed a glider pauses
between tilts
resting on open secrets.

EARLY MAY

Suddenly the morning pulls
open all its wide doors.
"Hurry up - I've already
let five of your decades
through." I try to hurry but
stop short: yesterday's still
all around me, wind at work
on the fjord. One second
and waves are grain in old wood.
Three, they're living muscle.
The green haze of young birch shines
in through salt-stained windows.

SUMMER IN THE MOUNTAINS

An invisible warbler
chips away at stubborn mist.

The mist is abruptly gone
leaving no inheritance.

Sun and drought in place again.
The pines, their sticky handshakes.

My body, three dimensions.
My shadow, two. My chattels.

BETWEEN HANSEATIC FACADES

Footsteps, pebble-tons on a shore.
Each wave sifts its chosen many.

The sea stops. The thunder begins
breaking every bone in the air.

The thunder stops. Then bells begin
pounding the air back into place.

Joy after terror. A clean tide
tugs at new burdens of footsteps.

OLD EDINBURGH FACADES

They keep rushing me into a future.

Each window intent on its store
of weather.
Each back turned on me as I face
its blind height.

I have carried them for decades.
Those weightless tons inhabit me.

I expected them to stay put
like blunt rocks in a nervous stream.

Some offer of resistance from my past.

LIVING-SPACE

    I

"Through high-up stone-wall country" - such exiled
words to read halfway across the North Sea
where no-one can pace out a foundation.
The waves add cubits to themselves and fall.

    II

House-fronts that hid behind the horizon
have rushed at me with the speed of light and
stopped short. They crowd me in, want me to see
horizons in a paint-flake, a pine-knot.

TRAVELLING ON ALL SAINTS' DAY

All those rustling braille-fingers
were still finding much to read
in the dawn wind. Then at night
behind crowding roofs crowding
windmill blades sliced up darkness.

WELCOMING SWIFTS

Weeks have walked past with their eyes down.
I've had no title on my spine.
A gate left open in the dark
opens me. Barley acres are
green and deep, rock me like a sea.

Swifts have homed in from Africa
to seventeenth century graves.
Serifs have not budged. The locked dead
are still open questions. Honey-
suckle keeps pouring its reply.

A CLEAR START TO THE DAY

The sun that has reached Finland is not
yet here: here we have Norwegian pre-
dawn steel brightness.
I look for and find Japanese-like
signs black on silver so razor-edged
I can't read them.

The sycamore has lost all its leaves
but clutters the sky with black-winged seeds
that won't let go.
The sky is cluttered also by crows
a creaking armada that lasts two
minutes, is gone.

I carry that taint of clarity
into the day's tunnel whose colours
go wet and run.
I have something sharp to interpret:
crows that have forgotten how to fly,
seeds that have flown.

CROSSING INTO NOVEMBER

My foot stubbed on a raised edge of rock
where two unyielding time-zones mis-matched.

An unfamiliar tense jarred me.
Pluperfect stepped out of the future.

My name had question-marks at "born" "died"
and a rough guess after "floruit."

That rock refused to be forgotten.
The first snowflakes of a new winter

spent the whole day not quite completing
manic circles, not quite touching down.

PRAISE

As if the ocean had written each note
of its rustling and knew its works by heart.

The horizon gives, the horizon takes
away, I have human eyes and can't see

the procession at its microscopic
start. I have human ears and can't hear its

variations on silence. Suddenly
as if I'd slept while waiting they're on me.

The swollen faces many times life size.
The voices like last trumpets full of joy.

I am too wide awake to waken up.
They can't come closer to me yet they do.

Too bright for eyes but my eyes are not blind.
Too loud for ears but my ears are not deaf.

In the glory of flesh outdoing itself
ALL FLESH they thunder round me IS AS GRASS.

THE HISTORY OF A MORNING

In the mind of the young birch
there is one direction: up.
The topmost twig though has no
designs on blue space between
itself and the young rootless
cloud hardly able to keep
its headlong shape in one piece.

Crowding bootprints on packed snow
have had maximum choice, have
tried out every direction.
Hieroglyphs break into each
other's small territory.
Firm evidence to read from.
The sun feels over soft braille.

A SYMPHONY BEGINS

Those straight lines into the past
fail to keep me in order.
The days I've lived through persist
with their semicircle, all
hold the same distance from me.

The last notes (now remote as
village lights behind black hills)
will incandesce, their mirror
will give us the beginning
like an old face young again.

The first notes, now, sound as if
they have lived through a long time.
Quiet thunder. Twice. Coolness
under heavy trees. Young and
old depart for their futures.

CLOSING SCENE

Frightened, brave, her last strength remote
as the blurred low-tide water-line.

She puts words to the wind's music -
"No house is too narrow for me."

He wades waist deep in bracken rust
perplexed at the generous hand

that takes. With what sleight of spirit
the wind sets hay slopes pouring up.

Sudden rapids of hazel leaves.
Quick indigo fans on the kyle.

CROSSING APRIL ON FOOT

The wind is a rough wall.
A blizzard of catkins
fails to escape its tree.
My footsteps are guileless.

New rafters have joined their
fingertips. Resin scent
cascades downwind, wraps me
close into a stillness.

My footsteps are vandals.
A blackbird's voice probes at
four corners of silence.
No wind was ever there.

TORCHES

About to descend. The shortest night
balancing on top of summer's arc.

The north is a window of clear glass.
The south is a window of smoked glass.

Between them I find two companions:
a full moon and a full cornflower

the nearly-light and the nearly-dark.
No opaque reaches can hide from them.

One on my left and one on my right
so long as they stay with me I can

climb down rungs to the cellar of sleep.
Pavements, theatres creak above me.

I wait through histories I can't stop
while my closed eyes refuse to go blind.

LOOKING AT MIDSUMMER

If I look quickly a sun is fixed
in its dipped skyline
like a Norman church, and a half-moon
is tons of scuplture
keeping its balance immovably
on a thread of cloud.

If I look slowly the sun bounces
off the horizon
and the half-moon is a kite and I
run to stop falling
down curve after curve while two old trees
calmly sprint past me.

FLENSBURG SPIRE

Three o'clock. A wedding. A bell unloads
tons of noise over car-roofs cobble-stones
and heads that don't look twice. It hurts no-one
as the afternoon is pounded and washed
away and assembles like a slow tide.

The shining cross at the top is empty.
It has the best of two worlds having found
the secret of perpetual motion
and the one not-to-be-moved point round which
local hills and centuries have gathered.

IN PICARDY

Labyrinths for pilgrims on cathedral
floors are still black-and-white and right-angled.
Centuries have failed to simplify them.

A gargoyle perhaps if he could look in
would have a god's view of the many dead
ends and the one contorted line of truth.

But he looks out, looks at but never sees
the blind woven roots no-one could undo
anchoring squares of sunflower, squares of wheat.

Only the fields of war-graves are without
obstacles. Their lines are unvarying.
The paths through them are open at both ends.

NEW HOUSE MADE OLD

Heart-wood dries, new pillars crack
and the cracks will be good for centuries.
Wooden plugs anchor stair-treads
grain set against grain to keep grain in place.

The empire of oak has mild
frontiers. Room enough for all those the dead
look through like glass, for those too
who turn opaque shoulders to the lost eyes.

My blind finger-tips read grain
memorise an untranslatable text.
The grain is live. The grain is
a tide I am too short-lived to wait for.

BIRCHES

I

On bare slopes a phalanx of dwarf birches
with open rib-cages instead of shields.

In valleys luminescent white sticks with
a confident slant
as if they need no guidance from blind eyes.

II

At sea: no horizon
only a place where eye-
sight stops, a ring that keeps
me at its blind centre.

A birch-tree would tell me
how fast I was moving
or with its shadow-hand
how still I was standing.

III

On the birch bark years have scratched plimsoll lines
against which events can be measured, like
a snow-crust subsisting on less and less,
a new green nettle-tide slowly rising,
me passing at sixty minutes an hour.

FACING NIGHT

At the end of a pewter day
the sky splits down at sea level.

All north-facing walls and windows
are suddenly elect and shine.

We're at the end of an epoch
or the edge of a continent.

As if to contradict me then
the sky closes. A tree explains:

"I am once more at the centre.
My north and my south are both dark.

I will have no difficulty
keeping my balance through the night."

Not for me to disbelieve trees
but I could tell him he looked more

the survivor when off-balance
his north gold fire and his south black earth.

FIND

Missing landmarks of my life-story:
they are discovered for me, like this
green pinnacle in The Pentland Firth.

Rock looks friable, grass looks solid.
The cliffs are sheer but that's where I climb
in dreams, always trapped, my hold tearing.

Family came here for funerals
in my years of absence. We're buried
in high graves only gannets could reach.

NOTES ON THE LAWS OF NATURE

I

Pines on the hill
chaotically interpret
the north wind. They brush against me
with raw silence.

II

Twelve blind windows
scrutinise me. That empty house
adds to itself one more cubit
of emptiness.

III

Monteverdi
abrades me with his present tense
his loud golden ignorance of
four centuries.

OUR ALPHABET

The way the wind defies gravity spilling up-
hill and setting free
quick darkness through corn stalks, brightness through hazel leaves:

I have written about it but it refuses
to become public.
The newly dead who loved it, suddenly can't see.

That unbreakable window we share with the dead
is too clear for words.
Our alphabet is open, it flows in the wind.

GENEALOGY

That rock shoulder - the eyes have
tested it and tested it.
The blind stone knows where it is
and stays there.

Is there a hidden anchor
holding the skeins of kinship
holding the valley? Here I'm
a stranger.

I stare through dusk: round the rock
shoulder a blind moon hurtles
knowing well where it is and
staying there.

DAYLIGHT

I watch from beneath.

The snow-flakes are black
especially those
hand-sized, hesitant.

The ground above me
clear as ice, I read
my mirror footprints.

They are always young
in their haste between
their future and past.

From my vantage point
from an inverted
invisible tree

I am old enough
to see the green weight
balancing. Today

gulls' wings are black too.

NIGHT VISION

An eye pretending
to be a window.

Flesh is transparent
but bones remember:

the strath held me closed
it was wide open.

Resurrection is
perhaps cold and slow

like waiting for new
forests to grow deep.

An eye pretending
to be a sack-mouth

jerked shut and knotted
with me still inside.

THEIR HOUSES

The moved and the dead had such
filled-up rooms. I would now be
an obsolete passer-by.

In a torn fold of the map
no-one has sold furniture
no-one has run out of breath.

Blind stone walls outwit the maps.
They butt into each new day.
I watch them and they won't budge.

AT THE MERCY OF SECRET MACHINES

They will make my last window light-proof.
They pour sight through my blind arteries.

They will shrink each picture to one size:
nothing by nothing. This rectangle
is not-much by not-much but it gives
the Ancient of Days space to lean down,
the line between his divider-points
a theme waiting for variations.
Trees and skyscrapers balance on it.

They will tug music back: it'll fall
like a string of beads without the string.
These waves of sound raise and lower me
freeing my bones of ancestral stress.
My memories are not against me.
The future tense loses confidence.
I am not drifting and I won't drown.

FLIGHT LEVELS

Two hundred humans vanish in a blue sky.
Not one of them could invent an aeroplane.

A giant kite saunters like an angel fish.
It can swim in air because it's tied to earth.

A spider counts spaces and knots his life-lines.
His copyright glints between rose-bush and eaves.

SUNLIGHT

It falls on the dead concrete
on the wood with its long life
on my hand with its short life.

A gull leans into a turn
that no map has discovered.

My surface is warm and bright.
My depths are for a moment
not so cold and not so dark.

The things that sunlight falls on
have a common ancestry.

One half of my brain calls it
emptiness, the other half
fullness. One half sees darkness

calls it light, the other sees
light calls it final blindness.

Let the brain contradict itself,
the concrete bury the concrete,
and gulls thrive without the word "map."

GOING AWAY AND COMING BACK

The brightness of the sea half blinds me
suddenly
after an avenue of gardens
and my roof
is now anonymous. I divide.

I'm out on the surface of the waves
and the waves
have stopped and forgotten to move on.
There are no
grid-lines to locate my lack of drift.

I'm under the surface of the trees
and the trees
have lost their serene habits: they blur
in their haste
in their resinous panic past me.

I reach home to complete a circle
but it won't
close. The doors I shut stay wide open.
Between walls
waves are running and trees are rooted.

ON TV
(i.m. Olav H Hauge)

It was the sound of his voice I heard
not the words
(which I lost) but the sound moved like steps
when steps know
which stone will give and which stone will hold.
His dead voice
was played again. He had re-entered
his garden.
On the night before his funeral
he stood there
(on TV) back to the camera
facing depths
of fjord and heights of rock. His trees stood
over him.
Their agile leaf-points covered pages
of bright air
with hand-writing too small to be read.

THE SAW-PLAYER

He sat under a wall of black stones.
Each stone had for seven centuries
kept

its place. His eyes seemed unobservant.
Each note he played was unsure of its
place.

His notes billowed uphill then downhill
now behind now ahead of his tune
like

a radiant mist. The crowd that flowed
at the same time eastward and westward
was

now already in an after-life
without knowing it. Neither voice nor
foot-

fall could break through the skin of silence.
The crowd went on talking to itself
went

westward eastward at chosen paces
along a present tense that had no
end.

That is what I watched on an island
before I travelled to a coast and
left.

I GIVE BACK SOME BRIGHTNESS

Summer is a present tense.
I am snagged by my decades.

One more weight has been added.
It's invisible. The sun

stares at the almost-weightless
and the never-to-be-budged

and both oblige with brightness.
My present tense tries to be

translucent as a thin leaf
and opaque as a thick stone

both at once. I give back some
brightness. And hide away some.

A spider's web makes the best
of two worlds, half hanging on

to earth, parachuting on
its fistful of half-held air.

FROM A SUMMER JOURNEY

Heat adds its weight to gravity
both pressing me down.
My journey is horizontal.
The sky is always
with me but it keeps its distance.
It is my habit
to stop and admire verticals.

At noon from a wedge
of shadow I count seventeen
copper pinnacles.
Their tolerance of heat and cold
is immense likewise
their patience in pointing upward.
They're all a degree
or so off-centre as if blessed
with the grace of trees.

At nightfall from a wedge of light
I watch real trees change
without changing into "Scene with
Lombardy Poplar
and Sweet Chestnut": the art of height
the art of roundness.
They share one labyrinth of roots
the spire safe on earth
the hemisphere touching heaven.

The night is not cool.
"Landscape" melts back to a landscape
I could get lost in.
In a dream I've reached a crossroads
where I'm free to take
opposite directions at once.
Leaves keep the dark flowing round me.

LARGE QUESTIONS

Such as time, and light. The afternoon plays
thirty-two variations per minute
on pewter-grey. White pain spills from nowhere
and bounces off the incorrigibly
unsettled sea. A man sits among rocks
with paint tubes. His brush seems to be manic
rubbing rubbing at a stain that won't give.

We're drawn to the edge of land expecting
and finding largeness, hesitant margins
where chroniclers definitively set
"Here began," "Here flourished" and "Here ended."
Marram grass roots defy shouldering dunes
bring them to a standstill. Nervous-headed
harebells, unlikely survivors, survive.

Tomorrow fills the space of yesterday.
The painter has brought home a small answer
a rectangle, a mirror, a blind-spot.
The uncertain harebell is now immense
in memory, overwhelming today.
A question has been asked, too small for words.
An answer has appeared, too large for words.

The paint has stoppped moving. No-one can say
if the harebell is nodding, or shaking.

A VERSION OF ME

I'm the one who
manoeuvres from "meanwhile" to "meanwhile."
Find one of me
on background plains crowded with cedars
and ochre towns
while the Virgin's face is a blind spot
a haze imposed
to give her peace from the centuries.

LISTENING IN

Briefly day and night weigh the same. Then
the first autumn storm tests the balance
of leaning trees.
It's still summer in the willow leaves
green with the flow, white against the flow.

Today, a blind ghost, I listen in
to a room where the gifted dead play
their music, sun
through mist, masterly now remastered.
I hear them two years before my birth.

DUSK

Not much height between
the finely worked top of the sea
and the rough undersides of clouds.

Not much light, as if
an eclipse of the sun now pours
its moonlit daytime over us.

Neither sun nor moon.
The not-much-light is not absence
but presence. It lets us see more.

In a dream my years
were complete in crushed handwriting
on one heavy page. I rushed from

window to window:
no light I found was sharp enough
to sting my watermark to life.

I'm not in a dream.
Round my feet acres of heather
glow: their low wattage fills my eyes.

TREE IN SPRING

The rock slopes are luminous.
They have lost their age and weight.
The part of me that can walk
on water could brush between
their silvery molecules.

Mist piled on the sea can't move.
It is saturated by
the sunshine it won't give back.
The mist can stop miracles -
"Touch me not for I am stone."

Between rock and mist, a tree:
still bare but incandescent
with unrestrainable light.
The blind part of me opens.
I watch the tree, am rooted.

The agile tree watches me
from many angles at once.
The part of me that can't walk
on water will be consoled
by astonishing opaque leaves.

THE SEA'S OPENNESS

Out in it
dreaming I'm safe in a wood. Ovals
of half-light read close-written pine-bark.

Dreaming I waken watched over by
oaks from Somerset, green cumulus.

Birches from Finland gather, shedding
on me that light of their own they give
off before sunrise, after nightfall.

PROVING

November has just landed
there in Suffolk meadows.
Ochre Norwegian sunlight
here takes a whole short day
to traverse "Suffolk Meadow,"
curls of ink, curls of leaf,
a paper landscape shone-through,
tested, not found wanting,
as if convolvulus turned
defiant proving tough
as a tea-clipper's canvas.

NOCTURNAL

Windows taciturn as gravestones.

Are the real gravestones transparent
and are they now blindly spilling
summer's gathered light on the grass?

A SIMILE FOR WILLIAM CROZIER

As when a December dawn
turns the undersides of clouds
briefly coral pink, and snow
newly and softly arrived
changes how we look at trees
and buildings, underlining,
in white, sub-clauses we'd missed
in darkened layers of text

so, painting Edinburgh
seen or reinvented from
Salisbury Crags, he made blunt
sooty and featureless those
top points, battlements and spires
with their long tradition of
catching the first and last sun-
light, broadened the lowest wynd

(with its traditional sky
ditch-wide and heavily thronged
by chimney pots and crow-steps)
and poured sunshine into it
enough to wash tenement
cliffs Italian ochre,
astonish inhabitants
with a slab of honey air.

THATCHED ROOFS AT NIGHT

Becalmed helmets, or animal skulls
asleep with their six senses awake,
war and humanity beyond them.

Among place-names beginning with Fen
poplars have the rise of gothic spires
pointing at the all above their heads.

Constellations have turned their brightness
up, they crowd in, light-years now arm-lengths.
The fixed stars are eagerly in flight.

BY THE ELY ROAD

Night between Longbeach and Waterbeach.
Headlights on the A10 - bulge after
bulge of brightness on blinds and ceiling.

Lights like manic pilgrims who can´ stop
who can´t escape from their present tense:
their saints´ bones are neither north nor south.

In an absence of mountains, small roots
are the miracles that bear the world:
wheat-fields and houses balance on them.

And those blunt stone naves we overload
with our souls, they will always take more
and refuse to sink. Their buoyancy

seems dependable out on fenland
that´s never still, as waters, half-held
half-free, almost flow or rise or fall.

ELM TREE IN FEBRUARY

Dreams of somewhere-else have come true.
I've travelled through five languages.
My dreams are as hard as brick walls
high and thronging me in. I find
my way among them taking time
to tell the shades between old brick
with its composite present tense
and new brick naked and timeless.

There's not a leaf left from last year.
It's an unlikely place for spring
to start but it does: waterfalls
of sound, music still black-and-white
too young for colour, but music
rough tons of it avalanching
through the labyrinths of an elm
I can't see, behind a brick wall.

FROM A HIGH WINDOW

Looking up. A bare ash tree
metropolis, no leaves, no
secrets. Winter light reports All Clear.

Bells begin. Discordances
claw at the edges of slates.
Every note contradicts every note.

Rumours, of life at street-depth.
Rumours, of standing at mid-
nave hearing nothing of the bell war.

LOCAL HISTORY

Mist-coloured cliffs become mist.
Distance begins at arm's length.
Beyond that, the island whole

now in imagination
only. It was in the parts
I found myself still living.

A watercolour of Glen
Sannox becomes Glen Sannox
becomes a watercolour.

By a stream with a Highland
accent hazel trees younger
than me keep starting a song

whose words I once knew. I'd need
to grow spectacularly
old to catch the rest of it.

Edinburgh's still crowded.
I recognise some as me.
We mingle, vastly distant,

hard tangible light between
us, a glittering choice of
"bright as life" or "bright as death."

Turning west from South Bridge Street
I'm a real ghost who once bought
blue jotters in Baxendine's.

Who would have thought so many
could throng Chambers Street yet leave
space for today's timetable?

The year's number plates date us.
My friend who killed himself looks
right looks left before crossing.

1930: my mother-
to-be walks from Minto House.
1957: I-

that-was brush past her. I watch
from 1996, all
of us like untouchables.

West College Street waits for me
in dreams, the Old Quad my house
of very many mansions

back stairs, secret landings, wells
rising from desks far below
where the dead are still at work.

I reach land. Through mist I see
the sharpness of gothic spires;
place-names ending in -cq.

MEMORIAL
(St Nicolai, Flensburg)

Killed mostly in Russia.
The accounts are kept open
in a side chapel, a vault
whose wine won't ever mature.

Silence in the nave like
banners that refuse to fray.
Silence that closes its ears
to the blast of Easter praise.

Easter has been tidied up.
Winter still rubs at slate and
copper. Snowflakes enter air
where there are no entrances.

ANCIENT STONES VISIT US
(Ales stenar, Skåne)

The colours have lost
their evil opposites today. Ghost-free.
Our grey cells are blue,
dandelion yellow and willow green.

Gravity has eased
the pressure of its hands on our shoulders.
Our feet have chosen
earth. They balance our unequal life-spans.

The stones have acquired
the lightness of paper lanterns, an art
of standing unmoved
whatever winds blow. They imitate stones.

In their present tense
the stones have no understanding of age.
We leave the warm field.
We have been here much longer than the stones.

IN MY OWN COMPANY

The philosopher I'm not
and I walk through Danish fields:
half-ripe rye seething, the most
fluid of motions, the most
unshakeable lie of land.
I forget to imagine
flowing rock, adamant grain.

Midsummer has gone half-dark.
Clouds stumble. Poplars are gauche.
A swallow with Africa
miniaturised in its brain
employs superhuman skills
alighting on the high-pitched
telephone wire, holding on.

The philosopher I'm not
and I observe the lupins
beneath the farmyard ash-tree:
how they glow in the grey night
how they stand still in the wind.
That's how they are for me. He
dreams of black lupins thrashing.

SOMETHING STUBBORN

I saw the universe
seethe like a herring shoal,
fish-backs fighting for space
in space without limits.
With nowhere to cross to
or from, my panic at
the absence of stepping
stones bridges ferryboats
was ... unnecessary.
Then I saw the edges
of the universe, rough
hacked wooden beams holding
the All in its place. Then
the universe shrank and
shrank. Soon it was a large
black spot in the blue sky
then microscopic then
too small for microscopes.
Something stubborn remained.
I couldn´t stop staring
at it the way we gaze
at where we think a lark
is hidden in clear air.

THE NAMES

Back to the Old Quad dream:
in the latest version
I'm on the outside of
a tall smooth column, on
a coiling stairway round
black doorless surfaces.
Will all this granite lean
one day, crack and collapse?

It can't. The Great War slab
of killed names anchors us.
It is dense like a rock
from another planet.
Its weight makes gravity
tighten its hard hand-clasp.
No right angle would dare
to be less than dead right.

NIGHTFALL IN ST MARY'S LANE

Tree, high as the roofs, admired
once a year for white blossom,
not listed as historic.

All day such crowds of the dead
blocking pavements, living crowds
have to queue up for each breath.

Such documentation too,
facts at high pressure, each step
as if on an ocean floor.

Minster bells kill the last light.
Tons of acoustic rubble
rush to test ear-drums, walls, glass.

Every brick in York suffers
gives back what echo it can.
The bricks go silent and black.

The tree now defies darkness.
Night and eyes moving there watch
an unwritten-on whiteness.

A BALLOON PERHAPS

Blue sky all depth no surface.

The loneliness of sunlight
on roof-tiles and brick chimneys

finding me out anywhere.
Here above ancient buildings
whose age fails to hide me, look:

at the height of solitude
sharp as a glint of mica
too wayward to be driven
too steady to be adrift

a balloon perhaps, over-
populating the heavens
single-handedly, then gone.

In a real crowd I restore
emptiness to the blue sky

my gaze all surface no depth.

CIVILISATION

Halfway across The North Sea
I look out: waves and clouds don´t
stop for the night, they belong
to no-one. It´s a pre-globe
innocent of Mercator
long before the building trade
and its need of foundations.

I look in: private cargo
ripe grain I saw in Yorkshire
at dawn, remembered tonight.
It was bounded by hedgerows
decades thick, acrobatic
dry waves swirled the grain as if
bounds had not been invented.

VISIT

Sunlight with no date attached.
Arriving, I am mostly anonymous.
Staying, I find names, become a restive crowd.

Leaving, I ask me if my
centre of gravity and Edinburgh's
might not once more coincide. "They never did"

some of me reply losing
at once their names again, losing their balance.
Sunlight on cobblestones a bright skin of ice.

LOOKING AT EARTH

Two or three of the vigorous dead pushed through
and stood on my damp footprints. Couldn't believe
my eyes, they said, which they stung looking through them.

That earth's colours had faded astonished them,
that life's boredoms continued in their absence.
"If you want us back you'll have to do better."

They were gone. I wished they had looked not out of
but into my eyes. I had just invented
a giant calendula big as the sky

to compensate for the shadowy evening.
I was tired with looking through a glass darkly.
Earth gave me a spectacular view of earth.

NEWS REACHES A TRANSLATOR
(For Circe Maia)

Twenty years it took from Tacuarembó
to Stavanger. It's still news.
During the moments it needs to be told
myself and its inventor
are so close our faces might well have been
illuminated by just one lit match.

WAITING TO CROSS A FJORD

Birches and pines have come down their long slopes.
They are squat and hazy. They swell and shrink.

Underwater stones are too visible.
They don't give a hint of sunless valleys.

Rain. Small rings hurry into each other.
There are so many of them they die young.

There is much of life in a backwater.
From here the wide fjord surface is opaque

as stone. An assurance. Sea-level is
the safest of places, height- and depth-free.

The ferry rounds a point. Prow and stern high,
a slice of melon shape balancing like

a junk or miniature idea of junk
in an old print, undaunted by ink waves.

I am daunted now, here at sea-level
for the opaque surface turns translucent

and sunlight can be seen losing itself.
The unseen valleys are truly sunless.

Time that has been running and running stops.
Birches and pines have loped to their true heights.

FORTY TWO YEARS

It's 1954, here I am
late one June night hurrying to meet
father who's waiting for me in his
black 1936 Wolsley Eight.'

Since the moon has failed to look smaller
after climbing to its cruising height,
since the moon has a whiteness to it
that seems to owe nothing to the sun

it's easy to be careless, adding
suddenly all of forty-two years
to my age, leaving father waiting
and waiting and I can't reach him there

unsuspecting in the sharp moonlight
under a brushy sounding pine tree
outside the gates of a Highland school
that June night in 1954.

PASSING THE BORDERS

It's not
father's history I come looking for.
The Tweed,
though, each time I cross it is his frontier.
His first
glance at it must have been Edwardian.
The shade
has flowed and the water has kept its place.

HAVING CROSSED THE SKAGERRAK

Having crossed water seen darkly
   and intermittently through glass,
having crossed a frontier not seen
   at all, now on the other side
of night only to find mist here
   too, morning welcomed by a bird
internationally known as
   Passer domesticus coughing
laconic variations in
   neither Norwegian nor Danish
perhaps assuming his two notes
   might be internationally
recognised as almost a song.

Having passed many lines of trees
   that have grown up expecting wind
to come from the west and now lean
   permanently eastward, having
found in the centre of Århus
   mist leaving a bright enough space
between itself and ground level
   for even the tallest human
to walk with unencumbered head,
   looking up though only to see
a cathedral minus its height,
   millions of patient bricks, gable
steps, big ones, climbing into mist.

Higher than which to be taken
   on trust as the gable steps do,
their way to heaven divided
   into one horizontal, one
right angle and one vertical
   at a time, assuming perhaps
their graceful way of ascending

    might be internationally
recognised as a spire, the real
    spire meantime, smooth and tapering
far above gables, lost to sight,
    today no day for telling if
a sparrow is perched on the tip.

ENTERING A FOREST

I heard
an ancient fugue settle on its root.
I heard
wrong. The forest slowed me down. I heard
two last
chords holding a silence between them
in which
two notes then opened like a seedling's
leaf-pair.
A fugue that will outlive me began.
That space
between two last chords which were now first
smooth sea
minutely written on by the wind.

ON THE DEATH OF WERNER ASPENSTRÖM

The life-stories: insistent
and many-tongued as the routes
invented by Highland rain
through heather. There's no silence.
The one-tongued river agrees.

One of the stories has just
stopped. His poems don't notice.
I think of them as standing-
stones whose dead weight is weightless.
They are outside language now.

By day they shed a darkness.
By night they illuminate
those who have lost sight of day.
Even the fluent river
can't interrupt their silence.

A DREAM, A WHITE WALL

I'm led to windows, fifty-five of them.
"Look at each landscape and be healed." I look.
Feathery cracks where the eye should balance.
Animals unnerving me with their speech
telling me I'll soon be back in daylight
with fifty-five new faults in my vision.

AFTER SIX DECADES

A ground-level world still. Moorland near sea,
heather-roots hard, harebells all finicky.
Above, indigo where loneliness swells.
Prewar, this sandy warmth rising past me.

ON A BIRTHDAY

If my eyes could slow down watching fire
it might turn cool
and gentle with its soft turbulence
its heathery
mauve like September hills. It might be
this currant bush
suddenly in bloom today, abrupt
newly arrived
immigrant so rooted here you'd think
the slow landscape had evolved round it.

SMALL WORLD

Considering the breadth of sunlight
and the minuteness of the lit half of earth

considering how wide oceans are
and how narrow the Skagerrak is I sail

northwards considering for four hours
the invisibility of land, absent

Europe that weight of streets and forests
last seen as a glint on a low Danish cliff.

CATHEDRAL

At the nave's mid-point
they've placed a mirror
for the curious

who want to look up
by looking down. It's
hard to see past me

staring but a side-
glance shows roof bosses,
miniature starfish.

The opaque moment
I hurry across
now turns transparent.

Arches point down, rest
their weight up under
arches that point up

and rest their weight down.
I stand where they meet.
The cathedral floats.

It has the poise of
a mirrored dinghy
on unmoved water.

BREATH

Seen from All Saints Passage, a horse-chestnut, past three score and ten
but much admired for its bareness in winter and in summer
for its fullness and for its vast multitudinous breathing.

On Trinity Street people seem to hold their breath balancing
invisible bundles, their weighty lives, on their heads. High up
"Domus mea domus orationis vocabitur"

on Tudor masonry, the chapel stamped 1564.
The rigid stone box has been rigid that long, a treasure-box
keeping its air still enough to let music show its muscles

then show its cunning by seeping into the pores of silence.
Wood rather than stone, oak toughening through time as if alive.
Not wood but a lung, inhaling doubt and guilt, exhaling praise.

INSPECTION

A gaze falling here would fall
on this upper valley's one
birch, rooted in the right place
to give tutelary shade
by a green mound that was once
ruins that were once a house.

A cloud shadow most silent
and smooth moved in but a gap
in it sent a ferocious
brightness, an incandescent
inspection - not on the tree
that lifelong customary

centre of attention now
marginal and in half-light -
but on an unfavoured slope
now featured and illumined.
The gap closed. The cloud moved off.
The birch revived its shadow.

SHADOW

Forgetting the brightness
that made it; remembering
the shadow, followed by it.

A yellow-hammer sang
"A little bit of bread and
no cheese" in 1940

but the tree he sat on
I have lost sight of, has lost
both names Latin and English.

The blank space between hearth
and grandfather clock won't do:
both sun and shade were intact.

My shadow without light
looks for light without shadow.
I could try Avignon that

summer when light between
high papal cliffs burned my eyes
(till I was cooled by dense mist

later on a blind hill).
Or I could try Uppsala
cathedral that dim Easter

long before open leaves;
except that there I watched dark
and light cross promisingly.

SIGHTINGS

I

The beaks of the swaying gulls
yesterday all pointed north.
The clouds were skeltering south.
At night a moon could be glimpsed
furiously orbiting.
By dawn there's no moon left. Clouds
are still skeltering but now
north. The beaks of gulls point south.

II

Ice-age scratches on rock as if
a giant grinding heel had turned.

Curves, sweeps, like a long exposure
photo of the constellations.

Neither. Late afternoon sun on
thin icy maple-twigs. Short-lived.

III

The young cherry tree
managed thirty leaves this year.
Yesterday the last
five hung there looking like five
ochre pears. Today
they're gone. A major event
in the life of a young tree.

IV

The hills, a thickening on the horizon.
The moon scarcely to be seen, one thin bright edge.
The sky, as wide and empty as possible.

No end of space for the fieldfare emigrants
their making and unmaking of abrupt clouds
their global swerves, their sudden no-longer-there.

BUYING A MAP

On the new map it says "The Old Manse:"
has someone locked up a house leaving
an out-of-date me inside it?

RHODODENDRON OPENING

Seen by me, as if how sudden
after such absence, fragile and
newly-invented.

Seeing me, from the confidence
of things that don't change, as if I
had been so absent.

ON A SUMMER'S DAY

Dreamt I was at a funeral.
The dream exits had been bricked up.

The sun's rays perhaps would turn black
unlocking all our molecules.

We stayed whole, though, hesitating
as if a well-lit after-life

had come upon us, to hold us.
Only the dead man was alive.

The dream gets on with its own life.
Hawthorn petals this summer are

extra snowy; pine-bloom, nudged, spills
reckless little clouds of pollen.

THIS TIME

The Tweed this time has forgotten
to flow, is a white baleful loch.

Midlothian speeds up. Poppies
are red hyphens in a green blur.

Edinburgh stone unlocked from
its hard centuries is a soft

flicker and is gone. Half my past
is whisked off with it and no-one

notices. My present tense runs
with the crowd. My bones are sandstone.

ABOUT TO LEAVE AN ISLAND

A spire shaped like a lantern.
An alley thin as a crack
between eaves, the many dead
of centuries step aside.

An oak tree a traveller
with a run of centuries
and no need to move - near it
I left a year of my life.

The Owl Nebula tonight
may catch sight of me, may not.

NAVIGATION

Native land: the Cheviots
a thickening of the line
that hesitates on wet glass
uncertain of its level.

The man with the saxophone
sends out a rough golden mist:
latitude and longitude
curve into a Celtic knot.

BIRCH IN JULY

When I'm feeling least up to it
(rejuvenation and suchlike)
there it is, a sky more cobalt
than I could have hoped for now right
above me and birch buds that once
in a week of cold rain and death
decided to become black stones
have changed their minds and are open
after all each leaf reputed
to be unique enough of them
with whispery variations
on the evening breeze to sound like
unargumentative rivers
at peace with their courses, that breeze
no doubt cousin to the high wind
shedding occasional cloud wisps
that follow timetables fearless
of depths below and heights above.

PAINT

The house that was painted white
was white on the hillside and
white in dreams. More than once in
half a century downcast
people left for funerals.

The house is painted yellow
now yellow on the hillside
but not yet in dreams. The white
dreams are homeless, they survive
on their unrelenting roots.

WALKING INTO A COLD WIND

I watch myself from a great distance.
My skeleton looks like rubbed sandstone.
A wind that has kept itself untouched
by blessedness blows through me as if
wasting itself. My bones are convinced
their opacity will not save them.

I look out from far inside myself.
I am on the surface of my life.
Something like blessedness blows through me
adding more molecules to itself
than it loses. My bones are convinced
now they weigh nothing, are transparent.

STOPPING FOR THE NIGHT

All day westwards unwinding
the road like a slow grey rope.
In our side-vision watching
pine forests lean eastwards mobile as clouds.

Let us imagine the pines
standing on roots. Let night now,
over-crowded and forward-
looking as day, keep moving beyond us.

Most echoingly the trains.
Most heavily the river.
Most silently a big moon
that stares at us in passing till sunrise.

ACORN

Sunflowers and hollyhocks promising
to open wider
in spite of the narrowing daylight.

There's a silence in the afternoon
in the most slender
capillaries of surviving leaves.

I hear it in Kingston-upon-Thames
twenty years ago,
before that tune you hum was written.

You also were there. We are here too.
I have an acorn
I took with me then from Richmond Park

evidence of a sort: in the hand
weak but in the mind
a concentrate, denser with each year.

ROCK

Here's water I can
walk on. It can bear
small faith and great doubt.

A matter of time
only, the age of
these grey and white whorls.

That other water
spilling in thin lines
has still to learn how

exceptionally
hard and slow water
if it wants can be.

My soul now - that flows
on rock and can't rub
off one molecule.

CONSOLATION
(On a painting of grass)

The waves are soft knives.
They hurt each other
most sonorously.

The boulders lined up
to mark IN and OUT
all turn their smooth backs.

Inside the room then
too many voices
hard knives truly sharp.

On the wall: silence.
Green paint not grass. Knives
in their millions have been stilled.

IN ADAM HOUSE

Thirty-nine years between
walking out of and now
walking into this room
the 1959
room still inside my head
remote and intimate.
If I'd been Lazarus
come back and tidied up
all the time I'd been gone
would not be noticed either.

GALE

Such hard air pressing all of Denmark.
The motorway is a thin wet thread.

Rainy cobblestones in Bishop's Square
have no choice have no eyes to close on
disintegrating anvils of cloud.

The church bell is out of breath. Strikes five
without the gravitas of echoes.

WATERCOLOUR

Four verticals, unsupported slabs
balanced on air, misty openings
on a non-wall, or sky samples each
with all the shades of a grey rainbow.

Cloudscapes seen from crumbling arrow-slots.
Papyrus scraps pasted where they fit.
Skyscrapers at a rainy distance.
Old Men of Hoy. Organ-pipes. Birch-boles.

In the gaps between the grey oblongs
three thin blue strokes, also vertical.
The blueness of the blue will ward off
pessimistic interpretations.

FOREST MIRROR

Mist has thickened into two giant pines.
They stand guard by a mirror twice their height.

In the mirror we can watch signs of life.
Blue stars not sure how big they should be swell

into summer skies. Yellow stars not sure
how small they should be pin the dark in place.

And then the crowding blue trees, their shadows
line by line, furrows on the yellow earth.

FATHOMS

Lights out. Downwardness
opens wide for me.
The weight of two more
deaths has been added.
I´m on a planet
with more gravity
than earth. Or under
fathoms of ocean
fathoms of absence
too much for my lungs.

I half wake, deep down.
Am breathing freely.
Words that are not words
have just said to me
the surface is tough
harder than bedrock
takes the weight I can´t.
The fathoms balance
to my left and right
above and below.
I rise into sleep.

OCEAN DREAM

Why do I dream so much of the sea?
Are my lungs not satisfied by words?
Are those all my verbs wrinkling away
sudden fans of shade on the surface?
Are my nouns beyond the horizon?

TWO TREES

Here's a public tree.
Like a fat post-bag
spilling its letters.
I wish it wasn't.
The year needs more time.

Here's a private tree
only five leaves, five
deaths. I shake that tree
to make it drop them
all five. But it won't.

NOVEMBER REPORT

Just before dawn. As if we lived
on an ocean floor.
The ocean is made of cold air
whose weight suffocates
our ambitions to be sprightly
and intelligent.
Someone's forgotten to switch off
a line of street lamps
on an unpopulated slope.
We can imagine
a thick wavery crayon line
deep-sea-green along
where a horizon might be found.

WE'LL LISTEN

Like the forgetting of names:
the skill of a single tree
to empty the universe.

Next spring it'll imagine
more things in heaven and earth
than our leafless brains could find.

SPARROW

I'm halfway across a second
when it splits and I fall right through.
Lock-jaw jams every word I have.

I stare at the shapes of "sparrow."
They're still as a fossil imprint.
They're a code and I've lost the key.

I wouldn't know where I could hide
from the onrush of a brown wing
that may be as big as a roof

or as small as a postage stamp
and that chirp-chirp is sharp enough
to hack through the skull I can't move.

The next second is whole. "Sparrow"
has zooped off - as if gravity
just there had hurled it up not down.

BLUE TREES

Above the blue naked trees
a brightness has seeped into
the blue clouds, it's lemon-sharp,
owes nothing to sun or moon.

If the trees were to walk now
along the blue horizon
they'd move with great ease, burdens
having at last been laid down.

GLASS

What's happened to the window?
The gothic arch still points but

the yellow stars have gone black
hovering like big soot-flakes

and the evening radiance
and clarity which had put

so many problems to rest
has become an indigo

turbulence, an opaque knot
of earth-brown, cloud-grey, blood-red.

Weary of transparency
glass has thickened light into

its own interpretation
of how a lucid day ends.

STILL LIFE

Life of a kind, never still
though the paint can't
move. Whorls of flesh, nascent limbs,
capillaries:
the cells have been successful.
Predominant
brown: deformations of earth.
At-a-remove
pink: deformations of sky.
A diamond-shaped
sun or moon - hard to tell if
primrose brightness
of such innocence could be
giving its own
or reflecting borrowed light
- a radiance
impossible to deform
looks on chaos
shines on the good that may come.

GEOGRAPHY LESSONS

I

Miniature Kent and Essex parting
as the Thames becomes sea not river.
A window minding its own business
at the wrong angle for me, cobalt
now then dipping to estuaries
on that live map whose scale is shrinking.
Blackwater, Stour and Orwell. The last
I see of land is the Alde's right-turn
just short of where it might touch the sea,
its thin miles southwards along the shore.

II

Five and a half degrees east, same day,
I am miniature, life-sized beneath
a pine tree, it too minding its own
business, its decades stacked on one spot.
The uneventfulness of its growth
is my invention. I give it, too,
a magnetic field of loneliness
with which it slows my steps then stops them.
I stare at the bark close-up: it's rough
mountain terrain glimpsed from cruising height.

THE WEIGHT OF LIGHT

Light too painful to see -
made bearable
bounced from a small mirror
then reflected
from a grandparental
varnished bookcase,
revealing today
hair-fine grain like
wisps of a galaxy
inspiring thus
my question: how heavy
is light? Think of
Emily Dickinson's
Collected: one
thousand seven hundred
and seventy
five rations of brightness.
Nine hundred grams
of the dark, of closed book.

WILLOW-HERB

Time to leave, when we imagine
the old white paint that was scraped off

looming through the hard new ochre:
indelible spores of sadness

in the wood. We drive for two days,
relish the thickening distance.

Spruce to left and right, crossed and crossed
lines blocking out sight and insight.

Willow-herb, though, has marked our route.
We follow pink verges. Seed-fluff

swoops on us, ghosts of snowflakes, but
short of the windscreen always lifts.

FUGUE

Two kinds of music at once.

One almost too slow to hear.
Forests have reached their full growth.
Decades are in balance like
huge weights that now weigh nothing.

One almost too fast. Quickened
notes like leaves in miles of air.
Numbered and safe. The tighter
they crowd, the more space they make.

A BOOKCASE, EMPTIED

about to be moved,
has come into its own without books. White
afternoon brightness displays the pine-grain,
whose flow reminds me of a photo I saw
of sonar readings from deep in a cold loch.

EMIGRANT SHIPS

The date is 1895.
The emigrants disintegrate.
The emigrant ship is dried paint
at one with the Atlantic clouds.
The walls that held their families
in are indistinguishable
now from the crumbling shore-line rocks
that become the stiff paint of the waves.

High up straths where rivers thinly
begin, it's hard to imagine
the sea. All summer hazel leaves
sound like a tune that has lost hope
of homing onto a full cadence.

The date is 1992.
A cat's-cradle of pastel lines
- bare bones of an emigrant ship -
fades into unfading whiteness
perhaps whitewash on a church wall.
Two windows blind, one clear lattice
with a crystalline miniature
of that ship from 1895.

We must be inside, church or not.
The light is too voluminous
to be coming from one window
or a wide-open roof. It's light
of the kind that can't turn a blind eye.

AFTER A PHONE CALL

Hazel tops are hyperactive
but only in one direction.
The clouds are churned white like crowdie.

It´s probaby Caithness I´m in
and she is much younger, her grasp
of time casual but faultless,

time´s grasp on her not yet so tight.
Her past tenses are still in the past
like wet clover heads in deep wet grass.

UNDOING A PICTURE

Here's a picture that attacks my eyes.
My eyes attack the picture, rub out
its title ("Night Solo"), rub out both
solo fliers (gliders or small planes).

The tall leaning tower has no windows.
Its roof belongs more to a cottage.
Wall and foreground are the same substance
green almost black in quarter-moonlight.

My eyes suffer outside and inside
this building: they fill it with six locked
storeys, the six decades they've lived through.
They can't see out of them, can't see in.

The line of sea beyond does its best
to be eternal, anonymous.
My eyes won't have it - it's the Fifties
they insist, and that's the Moray Firth.

LOOKING AT PAINT

Nothing black about it, this painting
of Lochan Dubh. Background, foreground, much
of the loch too are melancholy
grades of brown. The croft house gable end
is earthy. There's no house behind it.

A hill-shaped brightness, water or ice,
reflects blue sky above the canvas.
Tiny harbour, tiny boat, each wedged
on its mirror-image, lack a third
dimension where rope-ends could lie or
feet find balance. It soon frightens me

this Highland surface that may not hold
as when clambering along heather
back from Loch Araichlin, the parked car
glinting like a far speck of mica,
the two tall men with me now long dead,
I was abruptly up to the waist
in peat water, clamped by oozing sides.

IN SCHLESWIG

"I'm standing by the window where the light
is strong"
we hear him sing while round us all the light
is weak.
Crows drop carefully out of low mist, spread
metal
claws to touch down, fold and fold metal wings.
The one-
by-one elms stand alone in fields, leafless.

When darkness comes it is so clear that stars
crowd in
between gable and ash tree like the eyes
of shy
animals that have moved close to us, not
afraid.
The many-by-many, the deep beech woods,
leafless
too, keep their music loud both night and day:
it sounds as rich as any leafage would make it.

AT THE PHOTO-COPIER

A black-and-white mid Forties
Helmsdale. Bridge Hotel, Free Kirk,
Rapson's shop and petrol pump.

Telford's stone bridge looks so big.
Built to last, it lasts. Upstream,
the graveyard. How small it looks.

The village before we moved
there and those gable-ends chafed
unyielding sores in my brain.

I make copies of the past,
imagine I'm master of
sunlight on south-facing walls.

FROM A LANDSCAPE IN APRIL

Snowflake grinds against snowflake.
Grass creaks like old furniture.

I spread silence on the fields.

I bring home thick squares of it
to hang on my noisy walls.

LOG ENTRY

Course: 044, the prow aimed north-east
at darkness, the last light furthest west
low coppery. In Edinburgh
high windows in Warrender Park Road
will now be orange hurtful mirrors.

MUSIC FROM 1724

It rests its weight on nothing
and balances there. Nothing -
the most fragile - is unmarked.

MINSTER

Two hundred and fifty years old
the music they're singing, inside.

Outside, after much postponement
cherry-blossom has just opened.

All over the high walls silence
grit by grit is rubbing the stone.

WINTER MORNINGS

A slit on the horizon so lurid
we might expect blood.
It's where the sun went.

Half a rim of a new moon, higher than
last night and not quite
so nearly-not-there.

Constellations never seem remote, found
when expected in
expected places.

The astronomical wheels are complex
but the results seen
thus are comforting

like the manse Rayburn
kept alive all night, coals red in the dark.

LIGHT YEARS

The loneliness of a blue sky is extreme.
There's no depth on earth like it we could fall down.

What relief then, when night comes, to see the stars
once more, Aldebaran, Regulus, Deneb

close to hand like marks on my childhood ceiling
measuring how the day's last paleness took so

long to darken over the line of pine-tops
west of the manse, over the rise of the moor

its skein of thready tracks, beyond the moor then
over Kilbrannon Sound, and remote Kintyre.

THE WORDS FOR TREES

Midsummer tree-tops all lean
as far as they can southward
catching the very first light
soon after the very last.

From a high window I stare
across miles of foliage:
it moves as a calm sea does,
just enough not to be still.

I lean over words, not-words.
"Quercus robor" just won´t budge,
I think. Most words for trees, though,
don´t stay put. I´ve lost, again,

the Norwegian for elder-
tree while the white elder froth
lights up the Norwegian dawn.
The word will sneak back, leafless.

BLACK HARRIS TWEED

I'm soon to leave, again.
Ramsay Gardens almost
sways, light as a balloon.

I've left now, already.
Air pressure, hawthorn leaves
don't change at the border.

I feel Scotland slip off
like father's best tweed coat
stitched to last a lifetime

but kept for funerals.
Its weight made shoulders look
purposeful, both feet that

touch more firm on the ground.
Its weight was meant to hold
our warmth in. It didn't.

OF NIGHT

Ice has turned into
coltsfoot, tormentil,
trefoil, harebell, cinque-
foil, forget-me-not.

Eyes along ditches
close when night tells them.
The window open
by night is an ear.

So many rivers.
The sharpest-voiced, beech.
The softest, willow.
The most complex, ash.

When morning starts all
that's left of the night
is a vapoury
see-almost-through half-moon.

THE ROAD

Stopping for the night among birches.
Pendulous branchlets. Holding of breath.
Windows open, we at last hear them
rustle in excitement as they stride
unhindered to and fro in the brief
summer darkness of sixty-one North.

So may silences have crowded
the road outside there's no going forward
no going back. The road is not a road.
All day it led us, followed us, here.
In another universe perhaps
it'll be restored, take us away.

ON DECK AT NIGHT

Finding no moon, no stars, no
horizon.
Seeing no difference beween
blackness of sea, blackness of sky.

Imagining those few lights
(oil-rigs, ships)
are meagre faltering street-
lamps in a village long ago.

Expecting to hear footsteps
on gravel
then a knock on a green door
and a voice inside: "It's open."

A PHOTO OF LIFE AND ART

Taller, thinner than life-size
she stands. Can't begin one step.
Never will.
Taller, thinner than life-size
he's in mid-stride. Can't finish
it ever.
Stooping forward between them
a life-sized blur, a right foot
about to
touch the floor, two hands held tight
on a less than life-sized shape
humanish
heavy. A dark suit and tie
a smudge on the film, too quick
to be trapped
in sharp edges, trapped instead
in lack of clarity - but
what lively
haze! And impossible not
to spot it's
Alberto Giacometti.

AUGUST THE FOURTH BEGINS

An August sun half-an-hour
old has not yet come across
many humans to shine on.
Its undiscriminating
warmth in the meantime touches
curled-up calendula heads,
irretrievably splintered
glass, and the unchanging names
on Great War memorials.

SEPTEMBER LEVELS

Wedged clouds remembering at last how
to move, move. Autumn's contents are free
to find their own new levels. Weight weighs
less.

Gardens like careful ships slowly pass.
Each piled cargo could not be replaced.
Not one thistle, one chrysanthemum
more.

GATHERING APPLES

I revisit a field after three months.
Those acres of barley-hiss are now gone.
I invent a silence, try to fit it
over the empty space but the stubble
is too spiky. The silence stays intact.
Among apples, I can listen to it.
An apple-coloured moon, an inch above
the horizon, watches me. I watch it.
It's not yet pale, working its tangled way
up through high ash-branches not quite leafless.
Or the moon'll be still, the tree in flight.

NEW LIVES

On this side of clear glass a moment
has kept warm for seven centuries:
reaching the top of Purgatory
Vergil, who can "discern" no further,
crowns and mitres Dante, whose clean will
is now fit to follow. They'll soon part.

On that side of clear glass new lives start
too. Snowflakes are good at balancing:
they crowd together along thin twigs
and here's a tree of brightness clinging
to a tree of darkness. Two in one.
Will snow last like wood, wood melt like snow?

A scatter of black manic starlings
tumbles into the white day and out.
For a second they look like a splash
of notes written down by Liszt, ready
to unfreeze and drench with their rainbows
the black and white chasms of a keyboard.

POSTCARD

Blackwaterfoot from high
up.
That's where the sea was first
sea.
That's where the first bramble
was.
I have no memory
of
entering the flow, wave-
tops
by the second, oat-fields,
slopes
of bracken by the year.
Farm-
houses from this height don't
show
which generation is
which.

It's where the soft grass first
met
neighbouring gorse and rough
ling.

ON A LATE SONATA

Beethoven's fingers jab at the silence
which hardens the harder he pummels it.

Not the deafness, but a remote silence
close by, probing the music from beneath.

Outside, thundery rain is hammering
with needle-points against glass, leaves, flesh, stone.

Silence not noise punished the mortal wires
and wooden frame of his fortepiano.

Seagulls oyster-catchers starlings crows all jabber
at once trapped in an old madhouse.

Serene variations on the manic.
Manic variations on the serene.

Music familiar when we first hear it.
Heard again, raw, as if for the first time.

EVOLUTION

First, a tight line, a vapour trail:
those who are patient for eight hours
will be rewarded with New York.

We stay where we are, watch the line
break into cloudy vertebrae,
and ribs seep out - it's a fossil.

Will it now reverse history,
take on ancient flesh? Will the light
of original knowledge stare

down, like two primary colours
only two, of good and evil,
our heritage with no rainbows?

SYCAMORE AND BROOM

Little crowds of sycamore
seeds rustle like newspaper
above hot pavements. Traffic
fails to outvoice them.

Young broom plants have suddenly
put out so many blossoms
and of such redness you'd think
they must have needed

decades to mature. I'd be
happy with these but I think:
what a relief it would be
to know of the dead

if the sound of seed-wings is
part of what they hear,
if the warmth of red broom is
part of what they see.

THE RIVER

Such confidence in the sound of its voice:
the river can keep one statement going
day and night for centuries. No questions
ever. We can listen or we can leave.

I left but I still hear. When the river
has vanished into the wide Moray Firth
how could we tell which molecules had poured
with the overflow from Loch an Ruathair

and which had dripped quietly from pool to pool
of the hesitant burn at Kilphedir?
There is much distress waiting for rivers
who believe in water and nothing but.

A PICTURE

of a solemn man seated
at the base of a brick wall.
Unblinking in the sunlight
perhaps refusing to take
in news of a death, perhaps
no more than losing interest
totally in surroundings.
A picture that came with me
through Kent, through rain and traffic,
across waves and a border,
past Cambrai, battle landscapes
under cathedrals of cloud,
across a border and up
to the wide views of Hunsrück,
finally reaching sunlight
again between leafy slopes
round Laubach, each tree ruffled
according to its kind, this
must have soothed, or roused, the man,
who stood up and left. The wall
began to let brightness through
and soon the picture was gone.

FLEMSØYA

A December blast in June
cuffs the acres of thistle-
heads (we imagine thistles
are the sole inhabitants)
here, 62:40 North
on a small island from which
the best view southwards of wide
water and spiky mountains
must be from the non-windows
of a wooden house whose wood
long since turned invisible.
On rough flat land by the shore
stone steps lead to a non-porch.

AUGUST EVENING ON DECK

"Native land" is something I keep leaving.
St Mary's Lighthouse, and the cooling-towers
at Blyth, shrink, vanish, last visible proof
that a land mass exists, grand foundations
and small private sites. Our course is North-East.

This time we leave we're followed three hours out
by a deep inland warmth, the kind that takes
all day to ripen bounded by flagstone
path and cottage wall both centuries old,
while nasturtium tendrils waver past an edge.

BENEATH A BOAT-SHAPED MOON

There's no way in which a sheep could have climbed
such a pinnacle. There's no way in which
another sheep with a crow on its back
arriving in a small boat with big sails
and chequered flag could rescue it. One sheep
looks down, one up, the crow looks the wrong way.

In real life, a scene to run and run from
and still stand trapped in, like the animals
paralysed, with the fixed eyes of statues.
In art, a scene to keep returning to,
the improbability of rescue
encouraging inner calm and balance.

RUST

What would a blind angel see
in Gateshead? What would a deaf
angel hear if the A1
suddenly flowed with silence?
Because of the rust the wings
will remain compassionate.
Because of the wings the rust
will never have the last word.

For a year or so they stood
on a soft edge of Norway,
rusty men crowding the beach
all hungry for the beyond
beyond waves, another place.
Not even rust could obstruct
their longing. They were moved on
like unwelcome immigrants.

The restless journeys I made
for a year or so between
the foreign land where I live
and the foreign land I come
from began or ended with
a patient rusty angel
staring blindly from a hill,
patient rusty men blindly
staring from another shore.

HOMING I - X

I

Perhaps Altnabreac,
an excess of sky above
an excess of moor.

Always, the same dream:
it stops the train, lets me view
the place dismally

then forces me off,
tells me I'll stay here so long
it'll become "home."

In whatever house,
like a door I want to close
but can't, the dream thrives.

II

"Ben," "strath," "firth" describe
some of my notions of home,
feelings sharp as pine-

needles fingered un-
warily; sharp as seaweed
fishbox and tar smells;

sharp as coal-smoke gulped
on frosty mornings; soft as
rain misting windows

which end its journey
across miles of heathery
nowhere, homeless moors.

"Mountain," "valley," "strait"
will describe someone else's.
"Berg," "dal," "sund" likewise.

III

Three homes parents made.
Authoritative. Distrust
of uncertainties.

Seasons to trust in:
dahlia tubers lifted
stored dry each winter.

Berry-time the worst
possible time for questions:
topping and tailing.

IV

Hectic starling clouds
exploding and imploding
over south Denmark.

Creaking lines of geese
too. People try to count them.
For a safety-line

some birds have changed route
to take in the long new bridge
over Storebælt.

When does their "homing"
instinct take them "home" and when
"away?" Africa

and Sweden are tucked
up in their brains. Africa
is not "Africa"

and Sweden is not
"Sweden." In our brains, ours, "home"
and "abroad" waver.

    V

In my home country
the present tense is greedy.
It won´t wait for me.

Each time I go back
I´m further behind. I leave
before I´ve caught up.

    VI

"I´m going home tonight."
Told as a matter of fact.
"I´ve done what I can

here. Dad will fetch me."
Dad, her Dad, was heavy, hard
at times. Had been dead

for thirty-five years.
The word "home" a survivor
with no fixed address

gave her an address
of sorts beyond her prison
her room with no view.

Not the homes she'd made
in Helmsdale, Clarkston, Shiskine
but back in Thurso

as a child. Recent
decades blurring, remote ones
coming close and clear.

Twenty years ago,
arrived home from hospital,
father said to her

"What a bonny house
you've got here!" He'd forgotten
it was home to both.

      VII

Three homes imagined
by me, all of them now like
improvisations.

Yellow-hammers sang
outside the first, in Shiskine.
In Clarkston dry beams

in the attic smelled
spicy, clay in the garden
sour. North, in Helmsdale

winds from the strath, winds
from the sea couldn't keep their
rough hands off the third.

      VIII

Is it enough: wind
in the leafless sycamores
distorting all night

each quarter chime from
the war-memorial clock
high in its lean tower?

It's part of what makes
dwelling: wherever the wind
disturbs bare or full

branches, wherever
a tree can intercept wind.
We can hear breathing.

Tree-breath or wind-breath
or both. Our own breathing knows
it's not on its own.

      IX

The foreign country
I live in remains foreign.
My native country

each time I go back
becomes less foreign slowly.
It's not used to me.

      X

A rainy window
at night smudges all the street-
lamps I can see west

to Tananger and
south to Sola. What I see
is a photo of

a wide galaxy
each bright haze uncountable
suns. On a far edge

if I could see it
I would recognise that faint
constellation. I'd

read it like a map
river-mouth, harbour, street-names
(Dunrobin, Trentham

Strathnaver, estates
of the Duke who built Helmsdale).
The streets make me think

of the rough twigs rooks
bend into nests in the high
sway of sycamores.

The nests look short-lived,
improvisatory - tend
to outlive, swaying.

MIST

Grateful to the mist for
concentrating my mind
on the sharp stars,

on the pictures that ride
through the heavens and hold
earth in place; for

keeping blue a blue sky
from sixty years ago
one summer's day

when the sadness of death
- one death - as first felt by
a five-year-old

filled the known universe
the way elusive air
fills everywhere.

WEATHER-COCK

Not pastoral at all this
growl of February wind
through the bare wiry ash-tree.
The window has forgotten
summer's waterfall of leaves.
I see no sky, only depth.
The lines joining stars are gone.
There are no constellations:
each star is private, hard-faced,
sharp, inquisitorial.

Morning now - such confidence
around me: unfailing blue
surface that knows there's nothing
deeper in the universe.
Weather-cock unfaltering
on the brick spire's needle-point,
shimmering in the knowledge
that in its four centuries
there hasn't been one second
not dazzled by its glitter.

FIELD IN SPRING

Particulars arrive in a brash crowd.
Pica pica hops, picks half a squabble
with Corvus frugilegus and Larus
fuscus. Virtuosity is called for:
mortal wings tumble up then flutter down.
In their dull background Pinus sylvestris
and Picea abies don't stir one
twig-tip. Ideals tease us. Do they hide
when particulars die? Taraxacum
has patience of its own: will wait all year
for the field to throng - with dandelions.

IN YORK MINSTER

Borges became a shade in York Minster,
facing shades, fancying only the past
is real. I'd imagine the past held firm
here by a living vanishing present
now, a non-time, in no tense, where we live.

Slabs of air even on calm days dislodge
each other round those centuries of stone.
They balance weight and seeming weightlessness.
Two candles are lit and left to burn out.
Each flame is a snowdrop no wind can harm.

DISTANCES

Fifty years ago beneath the slopes
of Beinn a Bhragaidh - there they told us
of cool mists and ponderous apple
harvests in Tasmania. Also
of Caesar's steady progress through Gaul.

They marched us through the conjugations
and declensions, not one glance given
to the Latin names rustling and sweet
outside the windows. No-one explained
the Gaelic names balanced on each hill.

Distance in space and time gave value.
Has my universe been shrinking since?
The paths criss-crossing it take longer:
on each side more and more crowds up to me
like the calm heads of animals watching.

SPRING GALE

Rooks and gulls turn into rags,
make an effort, turn into
rooks and gulls. Tulips lose flaps
one at a time and are gone.
Too bad for thready seedlings.

Worst for me the high-pitched wind
cutting metal (but not) where
verandah windows don't fit:
the sound is a wire stretched back
across the sea and decades

to manse windows in the dark
meeting gales at the strath's end.
The wire tightens in my brain
which can't tell what is tugging:
an anchor or a shackle.

REACHING HELMSDALE

If it weren't for
this red tweed jacket
I bought in Brora
I might well wonder
if we'd ever gone
north of Inverness.

We shouldn't need proof
but do, it not being
normal to crowd in
so many slow years
to three or four hours
cuffed by a sea-wind

and buffeted by
non-highland music
from the Highand Games
up on Castle Park
(now called Cowper Park
after a merchant).

We'd come a long way
to look at gravestones:
we could read father
was "devoted" while
mother was "beloved."
Weren't both "beloved?"

Wandering I saw
Andrew Rutherford
had four doctorates
(honorary) chipped
on his stone. And Nan
MacLeod my once fierce

maths teacher, mother's
best friend and bête noire,
had an out-of-place
middle name: Percy.
Her mother Lizzie
sat by a peat fire

trapped and arthritic.
Unmoving headstones
turn their backs on us.
Blind they look through us.
This brash easterly
from the Moray Firth

is not going to stop:
the longer it comes
to blow in my mind
the harder it will
tug at my coat-sleeves
my hair my eyelids.

SYCAMORES

I have watched them from whatever angle
for years in real life decades in my mind
never as today
looking at them now up from the graveyard
watching the green whorls of foliage close
in and round as if
caressing, to hide from me, fold away
in their unfolding, denser with each year
and sounding like sea,
ice-house, Station Brae, war memorial,
belfry, slates and lead on the high manse roof:
it was the closest
I'd come, in a place always to me un-
blest, to a blessing, tangible and loud.

A KIND OF CLEARANCE

A baleful searchlight in my brain
fingered and fingered at manse walls,
at Station Brae, at Telford's bridge,
at the queasy high-tide lines green
along the queasy harbour sides.

The village was claustrophobic:
molecules in its crowded air
seem to have found more elbow-room.
The strath was agoraphobic:
molecules in its empty air
seem to keep closer company.

A wall more than fifty years thick
is no longer wall. It is mist.
As I walk through it, the mist clears.
An everyday river invents
its million ways round little stones.

DUTCH, 17th CENTURY

The martyr's forgiving stare, of course,
and the merchant's costly haze of fur
and the glint of sliced cod, partridge blood.

And inn scenes - but here at a distance,
horses, travellers, drinkers bunched up
to the right. A skyline waits for them:

if they were not trapped in the picture
they'd laboriously disappear
where inhumanly wide fields and sky

pretend to meet. The frame holds us all.
Far left, under a huge hat, bent on
his lonely anonymous journey

at this moment stomping past a low
leafless badly pollarded willow,
not glancing at the inn, a figure

too minor to be given features.
His non-importance, on a margin,
compels me to keep staring at him:

he softly takes over the picture
moves into the centre and traps me
making his private frame my frame too.

IN FAIRFAX STREET

The bricks are prisoners.
They are locked in walls
millions of them, lost
like Calvinist souls
who chose the wrong path.

Listen - like storm clouds
on speeded-up film
those huge spongy peals
from the cathedral
arrive and pummel

street after street. One
day, long-suffering
brick will dissolve, wash
over us, a wave
of sounds spiralling

into narrower
ever more subtle
remote harmonics
beyond the hearing
even of angels.

ON AN OLD PAVEMENT

Can we feel tenses?
Is the present tense for example
flat? Walking on smooth
up-to-date paving stones I stumble
as the road narrows
and ages beneath a preserved arch.
The paving stones curve
and reveal subtle grain like wet wood.
Are the past tenses
variously rounded, carved, sanded
till they are seamless?
Off-level I'm walking on water
and getting the hang
of not quite falling while the tenses
change more and more as I step on them.

BACK DOOR

Victorian back-alley, bricked up
and boxed in. One little box per house.
Into each brick box

minster bells now and then pack echoes
but they spill out unruly as fish.
Now and then a black-

bird stops by, picks twelve ochre berries.
Today a gale from The German Bight
has scattered big gloves

from horse-chestnuts. Even in the dark
hectic low clouds won't give up chasing
deadlines they can't keep.

An ambulance siren zigzags past
trying to stitch together edges
unlikely to hold.

OCTOBER DUSK

Coney Street at head-height still flows with heads
like Cuningestrete in 1150;
in St Simon's Square the year's first chestnuts
are shouted out; loud too in Davygate
by worn down eighteenth century grave slabs
the bagpipes wielded by a girl in jeans.
In High Petergate
I watch from a window a street so bare
humanity must have been scared away.
The darkest of bells unrolls five o'clock.
Huge amorphous blind presences stumble
poke at crevices between brick and brick,
give up, as if their fingers were too thick.

OCTET

Eight backs in the rain in a ring beneath
a sycamore, backs to the streaming crowd,
eight saxophonists play eight saxophones.
The rain can't stop. The crowd won't stop. The dead,
who have time to stop and listen, I hope
are delighted. I stop. For days I hear
eight glowing tigers showing they have learnt
to growl softly and contrapuntally.

CATHEDRALS AFLOAT

"There's no suffering
from which good can't come."
That was a headline
in *The Times*, boldly:
enigmatic news.

I could imagine
(enigmatic, too)
cathedrals afloat
rock-steady but not
on rock, on water

the water running
but never away,
the difficult light
and the easy light
hard to tell apart.

The bright webs they make
refuse to be torn.

THE KNOWLEDGE

What can we do with the knowledge no-one else needs?

A 1930s taxi, hot in mild sunshine,
brown glass with stains each rainbowed like a petrol spill.
The plates cars used to have, like SK for Caithness
NS for Sutherland, ST for Inverness.
Austin A40s, almost an indigenous
Highland species: a class rarer, the school dentist's
Triumph Mayflower, Uncle Jack's racing-green Riley.

The clank-hiss of shunting up in Thurso station
heard down on the riverbank beneath hazel trees.
Hoarse LMS and shrill LNER whistles.
Once, taking a boat from South to North Queensferry
blinking up into the girders of the Forth Bridge.
Once, Perthshire pinewoods rushing outside the sleeper.
Once, at dawn, a heron staring into Loch Shin.

Where can we pay with the bronze threepenny portcullis,
the copper halfpenny galleon, the farthing wren?

HURRICANE

Not a menacing man but each Sunday
with some threat that belonged to the word "God."

From Monday to Saturday a tattered
gardener or dark-clothed caller on the sick.

Father-figure and minister. That day
of the hurricane, though, crossing the bridge

he was a weak skeleton whose knuckles
on the railing might or might not stop him.

Across the road I also was clinging.
I couldn't reach him. He couldn't reach me.

Did father-figure turn into father,
more-than-father become less-than-father?

I kept the questions I might have asked him
like smoothed out-of-date coins in an old box.

INTERIOR

Facing a wide-eyed
window, a small frame.
In the frame, turmoil.
In the turmoil, two
planks making a right
angle above which
"lasciate ogni..."
tells us how unmoved
that threshold is, how
constant that turmoil.

One rose in a vase
before the picture
randomly set there
knows nothing of pain
we call on ourselves.

Is the turmoil Art
because it's framed in?
Does the rose become
Art once in the vase?
Is the rose folded-
up Paradise, Art
a shimmer between
live petals, dead paint?
In the picture-glass
a reflected whin

waves for attention.

A CHANGE COMING

Perhaps a big one. Hard to imagine
lengths of wool being able to shred themselves
into such thin fibres as these cloud-threads
fluctuating from ivory to pink
combed painstakingly over half the sky
by a vast wind that doesn't nudge one leaf
down here. And over the other half such
minutely carved scallops and whorls pink-edged
mauve-centred - if a human artefact,
an impeccable sheen worked from marble,
life-work of a Renaissance artisan
to please his Pope, it would defy a price.

Comparisons make me blind to the sky.
In my mind's brief absence from it, high air
has allowed to seep through all of its pores
an opaqueness fluctuating only
from grey to grey. A window facing south
has closed. Another, facing north, has opened.

ABOVE DOVER BEACH

Behind convolvulus and seeding grass
we park.
We see not one scuff or rip on the Strait
to show
two thousand years and more of heavy use.

Southward
across close-to-hand glitter and far-off
mauve haze
the other side if we believe our eyes
is not

there, just as we if we believe our eyes
are here
in a universe with a homely sky
and no
looming non-universes to scare it.

Below,
waves arrange the shingle, each with a crisp
cadence.
The tide coming in balances the tide
going out.

GRASS

Isaiah called us a lump: ALL FLESH.
How many tons of it in his day
even the chosen sort? And if flesh
is subject to real resurrection
how wide will the next life have to be,
how many names in eternity,
how cramped the privacy of each soul?

IS GRASS: but what multifarious
great families our souls could belong to,
Fescues, Bromes, Couches, Bents, Filmy Ferns,
and cousins like Yorkshire Fog, Remote
Sedge. With luck and elbow-room we'd flow
making of many of us one wave
stroking old hurts out of the hard land.

LATE

Bonsai nasturtiums
latter-day Tom Thumbs
end of season leaves
less than life-size but
perfect. Weeks ago
brown seeds dropped ready
for their raw one-in-
many-millions chance
against autumn sog.
These small hard green ones
will reach nowhere, neat
messages never
sent. Here's a thin cone
of blossom-to-be
blossom-that-might-be,
eye hardly opened,
waifish, bad-luck child,
an event too slight
to ripple into
the slightest footnote
in the fussiest
local history.

APART FROM ANYTHING ELSE

(like human beings) if I had to leave
for ever
I would abandon most reluctantly

all those place-names ending in —thorpe, -dale, -holm,
-ness, -ey, —ster,
or beginning with kil-. drum-, inver-, alt-.

Meanwhile I finger different words for "tree" –
Baum, dendron,
arbor, arbre, árbol and albero,

craobh, derevo. Some I can't hear breathing,
some I can.
Words like prayer-beads but none feel the same.

You'd think that leaves would no longer ripple
or rings grow
if I failed to remember a few nouns.

We drop words so easily, can't find them,
like farthings
sixty years ago, not worth much but once

gone, priceless. We're children again, astray
in the brain's
huge galaxy. Perhaps a grandfather

will stoop and pick up the coin where it lies
in full view
not lost at all - what were we thinking of?

LOW WATT WOULD DO

There must be a window pane
to tell us what's out, what's in.
There must be the sound of wind
flowing in at least one tree
without flowing away. One
distant light would do to show
how distances are always
to hand. There must be a light
beside us, low-watt would do,
to show our window is still
inhabited. Given these
we can feel roughly at home
in the universe, is what
we approximately say.
Then there's the sound of water
the quietest would do, small waves
where a still loch ends in sand.
A bonus, persuading us
time goes round and round, not on.

SPRING MORNING

First light. Oyster-catchers have arrived
from other worlds. Gangs of them scream, shred
the air to show that now they own it.

In the corner the radio speaks
briefly to God. The words tumble like
rash fledglings who fall before they fly.

Headlines follow: injustice sprinkles
from random clouds, old news, fresh victims.
I carry headlines out in this world

where I walk past an empty plane-tree.
The sound of the wind in it is full
not empty. A spirit descending

and caressing each branch equally
would be like this deftness of touching
that tons of violence could not deflect.

AS IN

an afterlife. Brick walls repointed
how often, a few trees recognised
now large-scale, decor inside so-so,
as in my time, meant to look not old
not new. In a gap between moments
that threatens never to close again
I have no present tense. There's no room
left in the past for more of the past.
Much has fallen into the future,
which never stops containing nothing.

It's an oyster-catcher - screeching out
of a present tense which leaves no space
for past or future - that breaks apart
this afterlife I'm no longer in.
Once more I'm hurrying towards it.

SHARED CLOUD

Anvil of sorts or snow-plough melting.
I watch it from out on deck - it can´t
be far off, due north. That stubborn edge

between sea and sky at last roughens
in the west, is now Northumbria
at its thinnest. Eyes on a hill-slope

yearn eastward, to somewhere not Sunday
not Northumbria, glide off the cloud
then, returning to thoughts of Monday.

Facing forward, I try to stare at
whatever line the blind ship follows
as if it didn´t even need eyes

to pick out a distant river-mouth.
I glance back: the cloud has cunningly seeped
into the pores of neither here nor there.

NAMES I'VE LOST

Look like forget-me-nots bigger
than Scots pines. Look like sunflowers
but blue, smaller than heather-bells.

Look like fieldfares but they're scarlet
as they zoop into - not an oak,
leaves too lanky for Quercus - yet
it has many mansions from which
non-birds may safely be observed.

At night look lkke constellations
whose shapes someone described perhaps
to Homer. They do their best still
to seem two-dimensional points
joined by lines which meet at angles
not even Cherubim could pull
out or push in by one degree.

THE COLOURS OF NIGHT

Have for instance kingfishers,
now that it's night, gone all drab
and marigold petals black?

In my dream the ship I'm on
and about to fall off is
more orange than oranges

and the deeps waiting for me
have a surface as frail blue
as the eggs of hedge-sparrows.

I don't fall. I brush against
a New Zealand Daisy Bush
whose leaves are like a rainbow

that ranges from green to green
and whose crowding snow blossoms
incandesce, warm me like fire.

On that fourth day, when the sun
was arranged, was there something
extra God saw to, reserve

illumination for dreams
saving us from the torment
of black print on black pages?

LOOKING UP

No wall is as thick as this wall of rain.
In dense air a distant landing light seems
stationary, a confused star adrift
from its constellation, no name attached.

I look up from a page on which Borges
describes objects he can no longer see.

Roofs are so bright they darken clouds and streets,
tiles pay out light it must have taken them
years to save up. They spend it in seconds
as if convinced such light can never be lost.

RAIN

The TV screens of all Europe show
severe low pressure south of Iceland
drenching Caithness drenching Sutherland
again. Water will be relentless
down smooth backs of family gravestones
and their lettered fronts not often read.
By the River Helmsdale, John Fulton,
father, Margaret Macpherson, mother,
their stones, as stones go, still unweathered.
By the River Thurso, grandfather
Murdo Macpherson, Elizabeth
Macdonald his wife, and his father
Murdoch, Free Presbyterian and
tailor, Joanna Shearer his wife.
By the River Helmsdale, at Kinbrace,
his father, William, Catherine Fraser
his wife, he who was "keeper of the grass"
at Griamochory, reached 89.
And then his father Alexander
who wed Ann Sutherland, 1801.
And the harsh sides of Morven sodden
again with more rain than they can hold:
I had teenage plans to reach the top
and get home perhaps in the one day.
What stopped me was not the gradient
but the unbearable loneliness
that would crowd in on me from the moors
and would stare at me and not say one word.

BORDER-CROSSING
    (Kruså)

No queues. No stopping. And the check point gone
that looked built on rock and everlasting.

In its place a wide traffic island's worth
of new grass, trimmed and not straying over
the bounds of the old site yet free to show
grass has its version of eternity.

In our version we wonder about life-
times of precious eyesight, decade after
decade in small cubicles, all used up
on blank stares, unmoving numbers, precise
personal details quite anonymous.
In time that couldn't stop, passport pages
hardened to an unrewarding surface,
an ocean paralysed from the deeps up.

DIPPER

The burn at Kilphedir, thin spillage
pool to pool, it was the deepest pool
where my then friend and I saw that most
nifty flitty creature as quick as
a trout with its suddenly-not-there.

That was the pool my friend went back to
days later and drowned, or drowned himself.
At long intervals his death hurries
past me, a private nameless comet.

Today it was the Dipper that bounced
in from nowhere. I could have asked: Where
have you been for over fifty years?
except, he is too fast for questions
and I am too slow to catch answers.

GLADIOLUS

Whacks to and fro, spindly stem gone mad.
Winds chase nothing across the North Sea,
barge in here and chase nothing on land.
They've no time to philosophise - stalks
are broken or not broken, that's all.

The plant plunges like that death figure
I saw on stilts: wild skull at roof height,
long rods for limbs, empty cloak bulging.
Before him, cleared streets. Behind him, packed
humanity of Bayeux, river of heads.

LOSS

Came home and found seven pines
my view from my north windows
not there.

The space they've left now looms more
than the space they occupied.
Between

my eyes and the field beyond
a thirty-year thickening
a blur

in the shape of seven pines
refuses to let me see
right through.

Could Ezekiel have joined
resinous logs? The magpies
minus

convenient branches wasted
no time looking for something
not there.

WORDS LIKE TROUT

in a glassy pool, abruptly
not-there as I stare at their backs.
I don't own words but I lose them.
Words don't own me but they lose me.

"Arbitrary" is a migrant,
erratic, follows no seasons,
most of the time hides somewhere else.
"Nutmeg" is wary and jealous.
If "Muskat" comes near me, "nutmeg"
gets lost in the air for ages.

They have their habitats, belong
(wouldn't they say?) to the Fifth Day,
will inherit the earth when we
step off, not one word in our mouths.

WHITSUN

Not points of flame but icy
tongues from the north-west sting me
by the shore. In crevices
sea-pinks keep their fine balance.

I lack both the bravura
of gale-defying petals
and the mindlessness of rock:
I could try between four walls

but so many languages
I don't know howl past, prise at
gable-ends with such fury.
I tell myself it's music.

Deep inside it I inhale
silence. But the silence starts
howling as well. A language
with only one word to rage in.

THE GRASSMARKET, OVERCROWDED

Down West Port, Victoria Street,
Candlemaker Row we have flowed.
What if the dead of centuries
had not moved out: where could we stand?
What if the next life has no room
for all of us, dead and living
in a jostle heading nowhere?
We live here forever today.
I'm one of the crowd so the crowd
wouldn't hear me, wouldn't see me.

Willow-herb seeds, white threads, drift in:
an outside world has found us out.
The living crowds keep on talking
but their voices send out silence.
The white seeds fill the air, dry snow.
The air fills, will never be full.
The living crowds turn transparent
as far out of sight as the dead.
The dry snow is not going to melt.
It won't touch down in my lifetime.

THINGS ON THEIR WAY

Last night an ochre half-moon balanced
high on an elm, didn't bend one leaf.
This morning, at the top of the sky
where there's nothing to lean on, it's white,
shrunk, waifish. It could say to me: "Don't
give me unhappiness I can't feel.
I know my way around the round earth."

This morning too I stand breathed upon
by wind from the sea. A small feather
comes not floating but flying past me,
against the wind: pilot, engines, none
but it does have a flight-path and knows
where it's going. It could say: "What are you
glaring at - never seen miracles?"

Is there nothing not going somewhere?
The ink on my birth-certificate
might do, it'll reach three score and ten
soon, hasn't wandered, hasn't faded.
It could promise to outlive me - me
a schoolboy still, late, distracted by
a seedling, a micro-sycamore
with only two leaves out. The seedling
could say: "If you do have time to wait,
to watch the next leaf-pair open - why not?"

PASSER DOMESTICUS

Loosened leaves soar. Crows, starlings, magpies
try out tumbling. Between two blusters
five, nine, no, fourteen house-sparrows land
sit with heads in perpetual motion.
I worry about their lack of weight
their sorry chances against winter.
Do sparrows look up The Chain of Being
ever, to cloudy superiors?

The most clairvoyant of them perhaps
observes my frailty (can't even fly)
and imagines a time when human,
house-sparrow, garefowl, pterodactyl
meet in the Heaven of the Extinct
shaded by a Lepidodendron
and watch constellations make new shapes
as stars in their slow dance change partners.

ACTRESS IN A BAD GARDEN

Stepping in, she lost her name and language.
"To be only me," had been her purpose,
"essentially me." The warmth of the walls
spoke merely of cold on the outer side.
On their espaliers the stretched pear-trees
seemed to have been crucified. She looked down
the well: all she heard was noise without words.
And far down, the mirror that kept breaking
and coming together again gave off
more light than it ever could have received,
such quantities of painful light, harsh points,
chaos confineless, no longer constrained
by those pentameters she had now lost.
If she had remembered Lear she might have
pictured his eye caught in such a mirror.

Stepping out, she had no name or language
waiting for her. The lines had been straightened,
the hand-writing undone, wool unravelled,
one line, one dimension, no end in sight.

WOOD ANEMONES

Days lengthen, spaces between trees
are wide, long before being filled in.
As if to tremble is to live
windflower petals tremble, half in

half out of last year's grass tangles.
You'd think they'd arrived from far off
before place has been made for them.

They are small voices, are so small
they know they have nothing to say,
are wise enough not to say it.

Each is too white to make much mark
on the spreading landscape, too cool
to give way as far as pastel.

That's the one place in the landscape
where rhetoric is quite absent,
where the landscape if it had things
to say could find ways of saying them.

LATE QUARTET

First we listen in, then we're in.
The world we move through
moves on without us now, beyond
a wall that's not there.

The time it takes, long while they play
brief in memory.
The journey it makes, from nowhere
to the same nowhere

an unmeasurable distance.

THE PROW

Deck nine, looking down on the prow.
There's no ship noise, no crowd noise.
The prow is a wedge of silence.

The world all round is small waves.
They can't ever stop. They break and
break thinly into hollows.

Waves rustle because I hear them.
They're blue because I watch them.
What would it take, someone walking

on water to glance at me
and prove I am here, not unborn,
but watching the prow in silence?

1943

Looking out: sodden green plunging from
ash, elm, hawthorn.
Looking in: see her stooped muttering
snatching Mozart
from a score inscribed to her, May Scott,
1890.
The window: a wet watercolour
running running.
A cadence says "That's that" and Mozart's
back in the dark.

1948

Rafters unable to keep silence
for long, settling
unsettling, warming up cooling down.
Out on the slates
muffled house-sparrows, neighbourly but
at their distance,
unable to keep silence for long.
Resinous loft:
beyond, all of Glasgow quieter than
rafters, sparrows.

1953

The Moray Firth is slate and sunshine.
Myosotis
is coiling through spray to reach harbour.
Below the hedge
blunt gales fail to tear young daffodils.
An inner wall
shows afternoon light, a slow reader,
fingering at
words on book spines, taking ample time
to spell *Cruden's Complete Concordance*.

FIRST LIGHT

Full moon at full speed keeping pace with me
on the motorway. Crowds of thin birch boles
lean forward, balancing, ready to sprint.

The dead we left behind in December
are in the dark still. They are so absent
an unfailing presence quickens for them
in this freshened landscape. They are now free
to outstare us like gnarled rocks, to hurry
like sudden fans of wind on calm water.

My hurrying stops. The car I walk from
has never moved. The moon has never moved.
Birch saplings, all arms and legs, rush past me.

LEAVING

That's my "native land"
back where it belongs
behind a curve of earth, behind
mist. The last lights I saw were like
little weights holding
down amorphous dark.

Hour by hour of night
hour by hour of day
a great rustling fills all the space
bounded by uncertain sky-lines -
not of forests but
of peaked waves breaking.

In a universe
of its own the prow
sees nothing, hears nothing, intent
on that invisible line it
seems to keep losing
seems to keep finding.

A HOMECOMING

In my dream I told myself
that square mile or so was home.
I arrived there in my dream
in daytime but it was dark.

The yellow of gorse bushes
the whiteness of wild roses
and the purple of heather
glowed as they do in sunshine,
showed me what I came to see.

But daylight came back, the kind
not to be contained in dreams.
Locals glared. "You're foreign. You
belong before we were born."
Gorse, rose, heather had gone grey.
I was told to leave. I left.

HAWTHORN

West coast of Scotland, west coast of Norway,
the sun's rays don't notice any difference
as they touch down at their ferocious speed
on thin leaves that don't notice they've been hit.

Here's hawthorn on a Hafrsfjord back lane.
If it could hear me I'd say something like –
as a hawthorn you're fine but not so fine
and not so hawthorny as those I watched
walking to school from Torbeg to Birchburn
in the autumns of the 1940s.

If now this morning I walked from Torbeg
to Birchburn and stopped beside a hawthorn,
if it could talk it would say something like -
I'm too young to know you, you're alien,
I fulfil today, today fulfils me.
If I had dreams you'd never be in them.

SUCH YELLOW AND BLUE

Willow-herb seeds rush from and to nowhere.
If I had eyes to see I could watch spores
- more shapes than in Euclid - all flying free,
dulling air as if the sun were eclipsed.
If I had ears to hear I could make out
how differently the wind deals with one reed
and with two, and with one and how many
cotton-grass heads bobbing like white insects.

What if all the plant names were scattered loose
and lost, the fidgety moor now wordless?
The plants would hardly notice, but I would:
creation would crowd round ambushing me
with such yellow and blue not seen since first seen
- long before I heard "tormentil" or "harebell."

CENTENARY

In my dream his centenary waits,
a crystal mountain. Outside my dream

we're together on this balcony
and I forget to ask where he's been

these twenty-four years and more. I spoil
our non-conversation by speaking.

"I watched the sun from here when you died,
watched something you'd never see again."

His eyes are sharp against mine. They mean:
"Who put that nonsense into your head?"

Doesn't he have enough syllables
to let his mouth ask how old I am?

In my dream, his centenary past,
I have walked through the glassy rock-face.

The crystal's touch is soft. A full moon
surprises me with a kindly stare

as if the sun had let me stare back
with no fear of burning away my sight.

THE BELL
(St Nikolai, Kiel)

All those postwar bricks holding
up new heavenly rafters.
The spire's vocabulary
has no words for "up" or "far."
The tree's vocabulary
has no words for "down" or "end."

A carillon splits the air
along and against its grain,
has no words for anything.
The sound-waves are light glaring
through concrete. It contradicts
the straight lines I have to live by.

LIVING WHERE

Each time I leave "here," it becomes "elsewhere." Between each time I leave, life there
expands. Trees stand still, horde their dark rings.
People who have lived for long counting
large numbers of small years are counting
now small numbers of bulky decades.
Even when returned to one "elsewhere"
I'm still absent, in another one.

This gale sees no difference between them.
It accelerates through wiry pines
that offer sharp but low resistance.
It decelerates through soft aspens
that offer uncertain labyrinths.
Far above the attention of trees
crows and gulls lounge. They have no "elsewhere,"
seem to have control of the tough air.

CLOUDLESS

Clouds were uninvented today.
The sun took its winter short-cut
from south-east to south-west, glazing
over the deep places above
with a hard tabula rasa

a beginning that would remain
a beginning,
tough gloss no ink could hang on to.

I watched all the notes drop like leaves
from the score of the Art of Fugue.
New leaves would never replace them.
Each page was as unwritten on
as it had been, would always be.

AT LAST

At last the sun has hidden itself from
the eyes and voices of humanity
and the moon has grown out of its phases
and now shines full on us, unabated.
High places are higher, valleys deeper.
Trees rustle with darkness inside darkness.

Celandines, gorse blossom, calendulas
discover how to turn up their brightness
and do. They have softly won over all
our territory, that was once too bright.
They've calmed the loud voices, the fever of
things glaring at things, people at people.

HEARING THE SEA

Heard my blood say to my ear, "just me,"
and my tinnitus, "I never tire."

Dreamt that Acker Bilk played a tune called
"Leo Fibonacci on the shore."

There were many crushed whorls to tread on,
a few perfect to keep and measure.

Does hubris make whelks build such armour
their lives in slime can never outlive?

We give the whelks a pride they can't feel
and a cruelty that is all ours.

What if a godless dark once huddled
in, died from, the shell of York Minster?

There has been much interpretation
of the not-quite-silence that drowns out

footfalls and voices between such walls.
It's like the sea we don't hear in a conch.

A DAY IMPAIRED

Began with green haze coiling
round willows on Fen Causeway.
The green was optimistic.
The haze could see no future.

The Stour reflected only
grey clouds that unpacked grey clouds
as if unfolding rebuke
over sunless Dedham Vale.

Ended out of sight of land
as Easter Sunday blackened.
Across Thames to German Bight
a blind prow could see the way.

STANDSTILL

The wrong kind of silence today.
An excess of gravity holds
air down
as if winds were not yet conceived.
Seed fluff of whitebeam, willow-herb
are as heavy as ice age boulders.

In a field whose green is near black
a buttercup generation
glares glares.
Yellow was never yellower.
If they had language they could claim
they defy darkness and gravity.

JANUARY FREEZE

It's coppery, full of August,
this quarter moon just clear of hill-
top, tree-top. And that's where it stops,
won't budge, can't rise, can't sink, ever.
In the half dark a heron stops
too, its wings metal, in mid-flight
mid-air, above frozen water,
can't fly on, can't fly back, can't land.

Why is it then a remote part
of my brain becomes immediate,
reconstructs oat-fields, lets me hear
the scrape-scrape-scrape of a corncrake
hurrying hidden in dry ditches?

WINDOW

Could I now look out
the way I looked out
six decades ago?

Miles of Moray Firth
glint and fade at each
flash from Tarbat Ness.

Or across distance
no-one has flown through
Sirius wavers.

What was wrong with nights
when the star was close
as a candle flame,

the lighthouse remote,
a spiky signal
a million light-years away?

ALDEBURGH PERHAPS

A heavy lid has weighed on Good Friday.
Cloud opaque as stone
is vapour again, opens for one star
brightening nothing.

We sail past laid-up ships sailing nowhere,
by day morose hulks,
now a lit-up city, a carnival
of light for no-one.

The coast if it's there is where life might be,
street lamps for instance.
Tired people are unlikely to look east
and not see a ship
they have no reason to wonder about.
From the ship, I've now lost sight of street lamps.

NOTES

"Hung Red"
This was the title of an installation I saw at an exhibition at Edinburgh College of Art in the autumn of 1969: long, slender scarlet shapes were suspended from the ceiling of a dazzlingly white room.

"Resolutions"
l.5 Schoenberg, String Quartet Op.10: quotation from Stefan George's "Entweckung" - "Ich fühle luft von anderen planeten."
l.9 Beethoven, String Quartet Op.135 (iv): motto - "Muss es sein? Es muss sein! Es muss sein!"

"Messages in Spring"
l.7 *Song of Solomon* ii 11: "the winter is past."
Monteverdi, *Vespro della Beata Vergine* (1610) V – "Nigra sum..."

"During a Final Illness" (and elsewhere)
"Nec tamen non consumebatur," *Exodus* iii 2. The Burning Bush is the motto of The Church of Scotland.

"August 1920"
J.L.Carr, *A Month in the Country* (1980)

"Icon"
Chagall, "The Bue Violinist" (1947)

"Lachrymae"
Britten, "*Lachrymae, Reflections on a Song of Dowland*" Op.48a.

"One-Part Invention"
Peter Huchel, "Keine Antwort," Gezählte Tage (1972)

"Two-Part Invention"
Sarah Kirsch, "Der Milan," *Rückenwind* (1976)

"Three-Part Invention"
Grete Tartler, "In the Lift" and "The Bell Foundry," *Orient Express* trans. Fleur Adcock (1989). "Vergil to Statius" - Dante, *Purgatorio* XXI, 130-136.

"Relearning Russian"
"waxy sputter" - the phrase occurs in Michael Harari's version of
Pasternak's poem "Avenue of Limes" in *When the Sky Clears* (1956-59).

"Equinox"
Dante, *Paradiso* XIV, 16-18.

"Inside the Spacious Tomb"
Blake, "The Angel rolling the stone away from the sepulchre," c.1805.

"A Dream, a White Wall"
This poem reflects my puzzlement on reading Sarah Kirsch's collection
Bodenlos (1996).

"Emigrant Ships"
William Taggart "The Sailing of the Emigrant
Ship" (1895) and Will Maclean, "The Emigrant Ship" (1992).

"Undoing a Picture"
Dorothy Stirling, "Night Solo."

"Looking at Paint"
Dorothy Stirling, "Lochan Dubh."

"A Photo of Life and Art"
Photo of Giacometti by Cartier-Bresson.

"A Picture"
The image of this man followed me for two or three days in July 2003 all the way from Canterbury to a woodland near Göttingen. He didn't bother me; perhaps he just wanted my unobtrusive company.

"Beneath a Boat-Shaped Moon"
Dorothy Stirling, "To the Rescue."

"Rust"
Antony Gormley's installation "Another Place," consisting of a large number of life-sized metal figures, was placed on the shore near Stavanger, Norway. His well-known giant metal angel "The Angel of the North," stands on a hill south of Newcastle-upon-Tyne.

"In York Minster"
Jorge Luis Borges, "A una espada en York Minster," in *El otro, el mismo* (1964).

"Dutch, 17th Century"
Jan Joseph van Goyen (1596-1656), "Peasants and Horsemen at an Inn" (1632).

"Interior"
Francesco Tommasi, "Inferno" (1988).

www.ingramcontent.com/pod-product-compliance
Lightning Source LLC
Chambersburg PA
CBHW022000100426
42738CB00042B/954